THE SCOTTISH LIBRARY

THE SCOTTISH LIBRARY

CONTEMPORARY SCOTTISH VERSE
1959 - 1969

Edited by

Norman MacCaig

and

Alexander Scott

CALDER & BOYARS · LONDON

First published in Great Britain 1970
by Calder and Boyars Ltd
18 Brewer Street London W1

© The Authors, 1970

SBN 7145 0178 6 Cloth edition
SBN 7145 0179 4 Paper edition

This volume has been produced with the assistance of
the Scottish Arts Council and the publishers wish to
acknowledge with thanks the substantial help given not
only by the Council itself but by its Literature Com-
mittee without which this volume and others in the
series could not be viably published.

821.08
M121c

Printed in Great Britain by
Northumberland Press Limited
Gateshead

84-3773

CONTENTS

Introduction   15

JAMES AITCHISON   23
    The Last Clean Bough   23

J. K. ANNAND   24
    Navy   24
    Fur Coat   24
    Mountain Pule   25
    Sic Transit Gloria Mundi   26

D. M. BLACK   27
    With Decorum   27
    The Red Judge   28
    The Educators   29
    Performer   31

ALAN BOLD   32
    Cause and Effect   32
    The Point of Love   33
    The End   33
    Six Dimensions   35
    The Two Cultures   35
    From Edinburgh Castle   36
    The Realm of Touching   37

GEORGE MACKAY BROWN   37
    Ikey on the People of Hellya   37
    Wedding   39
    Jess of the Shore   39
    Country Girl   40
    Farm Labourer   40
    Cough Cure   41

The Year of the Whale   42
Love Letter   43
Butter   44
Haddock Fishermen   44
Hamnavoe Market   45
Dead Fires   46

GEORGE BRUCE   48
Laotian Peasant Shot   48
The Red Sky   48
Fire and Earth   49
From Visitations from a War-Time Childhood   50
Pigeon's Feather by Sainte Chapelle, Paris   52
The Singers   52

TOM BUCHAN   55
The Week-End Naturalist   55
The Flaming Man   57
Dolphins at Cochin   58
The Low Road   59

STEWART CONN   60
The Orchard   60
Flight   61
The Fox in his Lair   62
The Storm   63
The King   64
Ayrshire Farm   65

JAMES COPELAND   67
Black Friday   67

HELEN B. CRUICKSHANK   68
Peradventure   68

DOUGLAS DUNN   69
From the Night-Window   69
Landscape with One Figure   69
Ships   70

G. S. FRASER   71
    Autumnal Elegy   71

ROBIN FULTON   73
    Essentials   73
    In Memoriam Alberto Giacometti   74
    How to Survive   74
    A Discovery   75
    Virtuoso   75
    Attic Finds   76
    A Meticulous Observer   76
    Remote   77
    Clearing Up   78

ROBERT GARIOCH   79
    Day-Trip   79
    I'm Neutral   80
    Did Ye See Me?   81
    I Was Fair Beat   81
    Sisyphus   82
    Brither Worm   83
    From Garioch's Repone Til George Buchanan   84

FLORA GARRY   87
    Village Magdalen   87

DUNCAN GLEN   89
    Ceremonial   89
    My Faither   89

ERIC GOLD   90
    Empedocles in Princes Streeet   90

GILES GORDON   92
    A Former Love   92
    West Cork   93
    Elegy   94

W. S. GRAHAM   96
    From The Dark Dialogues   96

7

ALAN JACKSON   102
    Young Politician   102
    The Newton Man   102
    The Worstest Beast   102
    Person   103
    Moon   104
    Notice   104
    Was a Shame   105
    Three Little Green Quarters   106

LAUGHTON JOHNSTON   108
    Willie's Shetland-Boat   108
    Fisherman   108
    Blind Man in a Basement   109

JOHN KINCAID   110
    The Backend of Politics   110
    A Makar's Tale   111

T. S. LAW   113
    Importance   113
    The Hero   114

MAURICE LINDSAY   114
    Stones in Sky and Water   114
    Early Morning Fisher   115
    At Hans Christian Andersen's Birthplace   116
    This Business of Living   116
    At the Mouth of the Ardyne   117
    Small Boy Writing   118
    Picking Apples   119
    Glasgow Nocturne   119
    A Ballad of Orpheus   121

DONALD MACAULAY   123
    Crionadh (Withering)   123
    Comharra Stiurish (Landmark)   124
    Ath-Armachadh . . . An Reusanachadh (Re-Armament
        . . . The Reasoning)   125
    Frionas (Delicate Balance)   127

8

GEORGE MACBETH   128
    The Wasp's Nest   128
    The Ward   129
    The Shell   130
    The Return   131
    Pyrenean Mountain Hound   133
    Alsatian   133
    A Myth of Origin   134

NORMAN MACCAIG   136
    In a Shrubbery   136
    So Many Summers   136
    A Man in my Position   137
    Old Edinburgh   137
    Flooded Mind   138
    The Red Well, Harris   139
    One of the Many Days   139
    Sounds of the Day   140
    In My Mind   141
    Milne's Bar   142
    Mirror   143
    Visiting Hour   143
    Writers' Conference, Long Island University   145
    No Choice   146

HUGH MACDIARMID   147
    The Ross-Shire Hills   147
    Facing the Chair   147
    A Change of Weather   148
    The Bog in Spring   149

ALASTAIR MACKIE   150
    In the Park   150
    Still Life—Cézanne   151
    Schoolquine   152
    Vox Humana   153

ALASDAIR MACLEAN   154
    Question and Answer   154

A Test of Aloneness   155
The Roar   155
Visiting Hour   156

SORLEY MACLEAN   157
  Curaidhean (Heroes)   157
  Eadh is Féin is Sar-fhéin (Id, Ego and Super-ego)   160
  Coig Bliadhna Fichead o Richmond 1965 (Twenty-five
    Years from Richmond 1965)   162

JOSEPH MACLEOD   166
  Florence: Sleeping in Fog   166
  To an Unborn Child   166

WILLIAM MONTGOMERIE   167
  Triptych of Miniatures   167

EDWIN MORGAN   169
  One Cigarette   169
  Frontier Story   170
  Canedolia   171
  Glasgow Green   173
  The Starlings in George Square   175
  From the Domain of Arnheim   177
  Summer Haiku   178
  Waves   179
  From Boats and Places   179

KEN MORRICE   180
  Brainchild   180
  Nigg   180
  There in the Mirror   181

DAVID MORRISON   182
  Dance, Glenna   182
  The Root   183

STEPHEN MULRINE   184
  Woman's Complaint   184
  The Coming of the Wee Malkies   184

ALAN RIDDELL   185
    Boulders Underwater   185
    The Window   186
    Failed-Safe   186
    Way of the World   187
    Breakdown   187
    On the Embankment   188
    Old Adage   189

R. CROMBIE SAUNDERS   189
    Interruptions   189
    Imperfect   190
    Derelict Cottage   190

ALEXANDER SCOTT   191
    Ballade of Beauties   191
    To Mourn Jayne Mansfield   192
    Sabbath   194
    Doun wi Dirt!   194
    Landfall   196
    West Going West?   198
    Summary   198
    Top of the Pops   198
    Marilyn Monroe Still, 1968   199
    Speirin   200
    Cry   201
    Kissan Kate   202
    Eighteen   202

TOM SCOTT   203
    Auld Sanct-Aundrians—Brand the Builder   203
    Cursus Mundi   206

CHARLES SENIOR   210
    Fulmars   210
    Triptych   210

BURNS SINGER   211
    Birdsong   211

Community of Worship   212
Home from Sea   213
A Landscaped Room   214

IAIN CRICHTON SMITH   215
Two Girls Singing   215
Old Highland Lady Reading Newspaper   216
Schoolroom   216
Aberdeen   217
In the Time of the Useless Pity   218
In the Café   218
Old Woman   219
Meeting   220
Highland Portrait   221
Tha Thu Air Aigeann M'Intinn (You are at the Bottom
    of my Mind)   222
A' Dol Dhachaidh (Going Home)   223
Poem: "Some move others"   225
Those who Act   225
To Have Found One's Country   226

SYDNEY GOODSIR SMITH   227
Late   227
The Kenless Strand   228
Three   229
Spring in the Botanic Gardens   230
I Saw the Mune   231
Night Before, Morning After   233

ROBERT TAIT   236
The Monster   236
Landscape   237
Scottish Country Dance Music   238

DERICK THOMSON   240
Cruaidh? (Steel)   240
Strath Nabhair (Strathnaver)   241
Troimh Uinneig A' Chithe (When this Fine Snow is
    Falling)   242

Clann–Nighean an Sgadan (The Herring Girls)   244
Cisteachan-Laighe (Coffins)   246

SYDNEY TREMAYNE   247
A Sense of Balance   247
The Hare   248
Elements and Adaptations   249
The Fox   248
Inevitability   249
Story for Imperialists   250
Explosive Dust   251
Earth Spirits   251
Mixed Weather   252

ANNE TURNER   253
Demolition and Construction   253
Medusa   254
Lapse   255

W. PRICE TURNER   256
Fable from Life   256
Personal Column   256
Select Circles   257
Reproaches   258
Road Hog   259
Driven at Night   260
Full Supporting Programme   260
One for the Road   261

KENNETH WHITE   263
The Heron   263

ACKNOWLEDGEMENTS   265

CONTRIBUTORS' VERSE PUBLICATIONS SINCE 1959   267

INTRODUCTION

The last decade has been one of the liveliest in Scottish poetry since the appearance of Hugh MacDiarmid in the early twenties. While no new poet of MacDiarmid's stature and revolutionary accomplishment has yet arrived, writers have emerged in all three of the languages spoken and written in Scotland—Gaelic, Scots and English—and they have expressed individual talents of notable distinction and variety. Although the powerful shadow of MacDiarmid's reputation, and the fickle winds of fashionable taste, have undoubtedly had their influence, to a greater or lesser extent, and with varying results, it is remarkable how many of the poets have felt free to develop their own capacities.

To some degree, this diversity is the result of Scotland's linguistic situation, which has a history as confused as it is controversial. Since about the twelfth century, the Gaelic language—originally brought into the country by Scots from Celtic Ireland who settled in and around Argyllshire and subsequently converted the Pictish-speaking and Welsh-speaking kingdoms of the north-east and the south-west to their religious, political and linguistic customs—has been in retreat towards the north-west, to the Highlands and islands. The Lallans (or Lowland Scots) tongue, which advanced as Gaelic retired, was introduced into Scotland by Teutonic Angles who took the land between the Firth of Forth and the Cheviot Hills in the south-eastern lowlands, and it was only after the Scottish kings had conquered that district and made their capital in its principal fortress, Edinburgh, that the balance of power between the Highlands and the Lowlands began to be reversed. Most of the burgh-towns founded in Scotland from the twelfth century were peopled by burgesses speaking the kind of Northern-English used by the Angles, and from those centres the language made its way into the surrounding countryside, until by the sixteenth century—when it was first called 'Scots', while Gaelic was down-graded to 'Erse' (Irish)—it had become the customary speech of the whole of southern Scotland and the hinterland of the north-east coast. An accomplished literature in Scots, mainly verse, had also been created.

After 1603, however, when the Scottish King James VI took his court south to London, where he became King James I of England, the aristocracy began to turn towards southern English, and the use of 'The Bible in English' in the post-reformation Church of Scotland made English obligatory for the discussion of intellectual affairs. Yet Gaelic in the Highlands, and Scots in the Lowlands, remained—and, although in decline, still remain—the native tongues of the great majority of the population, and literary works in those older languages continued to be composed alongside verse and prose in the metropolitan English which aristocrats and academics had espoused. In Gaeldom, the high tradition of art poetry remained virtually unbroken, despite civil war, subjugation, clearances and colonialism, although the delayed impact of the reformation, in the late eighteenth and nineteenth centuries, brought all art into disrepute except the didactic. In the Lowlands, during the seventeenth century, the art poetry in Scots which had been written by the medieval and renaissance makars for a courtly and educated audience was replaced by art poetry in English. But while folk-poetry—ballads and other songs—continued unabated, the break in the high tradition has never yet been entirely healed, despite all the attempts which have followed Allan Ramsay's prime endeavour to resuscitate medieval verse in his anthology *The Evergreen* (1724).

The eighteenth century revival of poetry in Scots, which culminated in the work of Burns—although it was continued, with individual nuances, by Hogg and Tennant into the next generation—had many merits, but the kind of intellectual passion which only the greatest poetry can express was not one of them. The subsequent degeneration of the post-Burnsian school into the pathetic, the pawky and the parochial throughout the last three-quarters of the nineteenth century made all the harder the task of recovering and revitalising the medieval synthesis of the profound and the profane when MacDiarmid addressed himself to it after the First World War. That he succeeded so often, and so spectacularly, is well-nigh miraculous, considering how the Scots language had disintegrated into local dialects which he had to weld together to form a new literary medium, but it would be idle to pretend that the 'sair fecht' (sore fight) involved has not left its traces on his work, even (sometimes) on his finest.

Although MacDiarmid, like most Lowlanders of his generation, except the landed gentry and the long-established professional families, was a native speaker of Scots, he began his poetical career in English, for by then it was accepted as axiomatic that 'elevated' poetry by a Scottish writer should be expressed in that language. The fact in itself may be sufficient explanation as to why the sense of 'the whole man' being involved is so intermittent in Anglo-Scottish poetry, from Drummond at the beginning of the seventeenth century to Davidson at the beginning of the twentieth, the effort at elevation appearing so evident, the contact with earth (and earthiness) so slight. That the case has altered during the past fifty years is due to the fact that more and more of those Scotsmen who have Scots or Gaelic as their native tongues have been introduced to English from the start of their schooling at the age of five, while an ever-increasing number have spoken only English from the beginning.

MacDiarmid's 'conversion' to Scots as a poetical medium for the expression of the highest (as well as the lowest) aspects of the Scottish ethos resulted in his writing some of the greatest poetry of this century and, in *A Drunk Man Looks at The Thistle* (1926), the greatest extended work in the whole of Scottish verse. But his creative achievement in the twenties was accompanied by a propagandist proclamation of 'the Scots language, the whole Scots language, and nothing but the Scots language', which has come to seem anachronistic at a time when increasing exposure to English has made so many Scotsmen

17

feel no less at home and at ease in that language than in Scots or Gaelic.

However, MacDiarmid has practised more than he has preached and has accomplished noteworthy work in both Scots and—more lately—English, as well in the comparatively few new poems which he has published during the last decade as in the many produced earlier. Yet the number of bi-lingual Scottish writers who have been equally (or almost-equally) successful in English and Scots, or in English and Gaelic, remains small. Most have preferred to concentrate on only one of their two tongues, and the majority of the rest show more command, or greater range, in one language than in the other. A grand exception to this general rule is Iain Crichton Smith, a Highland poet outstanding in English, who has also contributed fine work to Gaelic drama, fiction and verse.

Among those from the Highlands and islands who write in Gaelic alone, there is such vitality that it is difficult to accept the statistical evidence that the language is dying. Sorley Maclean, whose *Dain do Eimhir* (1943) made Gaelic contemporary—an achievement comparable with MacDiarmid's revitalisation of Scots two decades earlier—continues to write in a manner which is at once twentieth-century and timeless, and with a fusion of intellect and passion rare in any poetry. Derick Thomson's themes, too, are at once contemporary and traditional, and his style weaves together the old and the new. In Donald Macaulay's work, the experimental is more evident, and his example has been followed by a number of still younger writers who would also have been represented here if only they had not held the characteristically Celtic view that when God made time He made plenty of it—an idea at variance with the modern innovation of the dead-line. A similar attitude is responsible for George Campbell Hay's absence from these pages.

Campbell Hay, who has also written fine work in Scots, is an avowed admirer and disciple of MacDiarmid, and the same is true—to some extent—of all contemporary Scots makars, even of those whose achievement is most individual. Throughout this decade, as for the past quarter-century, Sydney Goodsir Smith has been the most prolific, the most passionate, and the most powerful of the Lallans poets, despite the unevenness of some of his most recent work. Among the impulses behind Goodsir Smith's *oeuvre* is the zeal of the convert, for although he is a Scot on his mother's side he was born in New Zealand and educated in England, and the Lallans medium which he has forged is very much an individual creation, combining vernacular Scots, as currently spoken, with an 'aureate leid' (gilded language) equivalent to that employed by the medieval makars for ceremonial themes, but owing much to Joyce and Pound as well as to Henryson and Dunbar. While he has attempted verse-drama, he is most successful when his protagonists speak with his own voice, and his swift and subtle rhythms and his cunningly-contrived stanzas and verse paragraphs, with their abrupt transitions and their darting and pausing, convey the impression of unusual emotional energy—and emotional honesty too.

If Edinburgh has become Goodsir Smith's adopted native city, as Scots has become his adopted tongue, Robert Garioch belongs to both by birth, and the vivid accuracy of its local colour is as notable a feature of his work as its idiomatic verve. In his sparkling series of *Sixteen Edinburgh Sonnets*, and elsewhere, the underdog who bites the ankles of the powerful and the pretentious is, in various sizes, shapes and forms, the truly dominant character. Another Edinburgh schoolmaster of Garioch's generation, J. K. Annand, has turned his profession to advantage by becoming a writer of bairn-rhymes, after the style of William Soutar (1898–1943), and the effective simplicity of his best writing can be equally appropriate to adult themes, both grave and gay—for all the Scots makars have the gift of comedy. A much more ambitious poet, Tom Scott, has difficulty in controlling an urge towards over-emphasis, but when he succeeds in this his work is outstanding for its synthesis of satire and sympathy.

Among the poets in Scots who have emerged since the fifties, the most accomplished is Alastair Mackie, from the North-East

—an area where Scots probably remains more secure in the mouths of the people than anywhere else in the country. Mackie's idiomatic command of his medium gives him a fine range of themes, from the local to the universal, in work remarkable for its directness and drive. More recently, the appearance of still younger poets—Eric Gold, Duncan Glen—has shown that the Scots tradition maintains its capacity to survive and develop.

Most of the younger poets, however, write in English, which has become the majority language for poetry from Scotland. But they do not form a group—among Scotsmen, groups are apt to be groups of one, and any backscratching is done with a dirk. This stubborn individualism may have its bad aspects, but at the very least it ensures variety—although many of these writers share the characteristic Scottish (literary) qualities of directness and lucidity; which means that when their work is bad it is noticeably so.

Individuality also preserves them from the dubious advantages of centralism—half of these poets do not even live in Scotland, and those who do are scattered all over the place. George Mackay Brown writes his tough, rich, laconic, passionate, witty poems in the Orkneys. Iain Chrichton Smith explores more deeply his old themes of puritanism, grace and good works and, these days, looks more and more beyond them, in Oban; while Alasdair Maclean's strange poems, often gruesome and witty at once, emerge from the agreeable fastnesses of Ardnamurchan.

Even in the two largest cities, Edinburgh and Glasgow, the poets disagree to differ. From the old capital, George Bruce looks north to Aberdeenshire and east across the world, writing with equal economy and energy on his own past and on the common contemporary predicament; Robin Fulton explores the meaning of meaning by combining paradox and passion in a style pared to the bone; Alan Jackson attacks human absurdity —including his own—in a notable variety of forms, from the stab of epigram to the macabre mythology of science-fiction; and Alan Bold attempts the epic view. From the western cosmopolis, Tom Buchan makes his taut poems from the tension between love and disillusion; Stewart Conn creates legends from his own youth, from the youth of the world, and from the present situation; Maurice Lindsay sketches urban and rural scenes with nice sensitivity and controlled force; and Edwin Morgan provides a one-man anthology of styles, from the simple traditional through urban vernacular and on through space to —of all things—concrete poetry. 'Of all things?' Yes; for although the Scots have seldom been remarkable as innovators in the arts, they have produced, in Morgan and Ian Hamilton Finlay, two of the more noteworthy of the concretists. We regret that differences between Finlay, his publisher, and ourselves, have left us with no alternative but to omit his work— both orthodox and unorthodox—from this selection.

Most of the exiles, or refugees, are naturally to be found in England—George Macbeth, in the very centre of the Great Wen itself, writes copiously in styles that vary from the traditional to the eccentric, while his disciple D. M. Black is either modishly ambiguous or unfashionably plain; W. Price Turner produces, from Yorkshire, poems of irony and passion which deserve more notice than they get, on either side of the Border; and W. S. Graham, remarkable for his verbal music, has broken a long silence with a book which regrettably is appearing too late for us to consider for this anthology. The escape to England and further places is, of course, a phenomenon all too common in the history of the Scots, whose chief export continues to be people, but is all the more curious in the case of our contemporary writers since many of them are distinctly nationalist in sentiment as well as left-wing in politics. But there is not a great deal of *directly* political writing being produced, and most of that—as is usual—is not very good. However, this does not mean that no concern is shown for the miseries and triumphs of the contemporary human condition. Poems written out of concern for injustice and pity for those who suffer from it may be political, but only in an indirect way, as the best so-called political poetry generally turns out to be.

As far as we can discover, all the poems published here were written in the last ten years, and we have tried to represent all the kinds of contemporary Scottish verse. The token representation of concrete work is due to our doubt as to whether this is in fact poetry—whatever else it may be. We are grateful to the Scottish Arts Council for a grant in aid of publication.

N. MacC.
A.S.

December 1969

JAMES AITCHISON b. 1938

THE LAST CLEAN BOUGH

Each day that summer he walked the avenue
of elm and hawthorn to the broken orchard.

He put his saw to the dry bough and he thought
of autumns full of fruit, of blossomings.

And he remembered a girl, a night when leaves
moved in the wind and moonlight silvered her.

But that was fifty years ago . . . Now
the house beyond the orchard was a shell.

The orchard wall had fallen stone by stone
and the fruitless trees had fallen: apple, plum,

damson, cherry, pear—the pear tree where
the summer moon had found the silver girl.

The girl beneath the tree beneath the moon
was long since dead. What had they said

that summer night beneath the pear tree where
now he put his saw to the last clean bough?

He shouldered the branch and walked the avenue
of big elms and sparse hawthorn hedge.

In his garden he dropped it on the pile
of timbers stacked against the coming frost.

NAVY

"What gart ye jine the navy, Jock?"
   My faither was a sodger.
He spak eneuch o Flanders glaur
   To mak me be a dodger.

I lippent on a warm dry bed,
   My baccy and my rum,
A cleanly daith and a watery grave
   Gif Davy Jones soud come.

I little thocht to doss me doun
   In a craft sae smaa and frail,
Wi hammock slung ablow a deck
   That leaks like the Grey Mear's Tail.

And little I thocht to be lockit in
   A magazine like a jyle,
Or end my days in the chokin clart
   O' a sea befylt wi ile.

gart—made; *jine*—join; *sodger*—soldier; *spak eneuch*—spoke enough; *glaur*
—mud; *lippent*—had confidence; *gif*—if; *ablow*—below; *jyle*—jail; *clart*—
filth; *befylt wi ile*—befouled with oil.

FUR COATS

Said the whitrick to the stoat,
"I see ye've on your winter coat.
I dinna see the sense ava!
Ye're shairly no expectin snaw?"

24

To the whitrick said the stoat,
"At least it's mair nor you hae got.
I'm gled I dinna hae to wear
The same auld coat throughout the year."

Said the whitrick to the stoat,
"I wadna mak owre muckle o't.
While nane will covet my auld coat
Your ermine fur wi tip o black
Will aiblins cleed a Provost's back."

whitrick—weasel; *dinna*—don't; *ava*—at all; *shairly*—surely; *owre muckle
o't*—too much of it; *aiblins cleed*—perhaps clothe.

MOUNTAIN PULE

I saw ferlies in thon mountain pule.
Its deeps I couldna faddom, but I kent
Ilk drap o water in its shadowy mass
Begoud as crystal on a slender stem
Heich on the mountainside, syne wi its peers
Whummelt owre craigs, mellin wi licht and air,
Afore it settled in thon lownsome place.

Sae wi your mind. The deeps o thocht that dern
Intil't I'll never faddom, but whiles there kythes
Ayont your smile the dew that kittles up
And nourishes my spreit as thon deep pule
Sustained amang the stanes a gowden flouer.

pule—pool; *ferlies*—marvels; *faddom*—fathom; *kent*—knew; *ilk*—each;
begoud—began; *heich*—high; *syne*—then; *whummelt*—tumbled; *craigs*—
rocks; *mellin*—mixing; *afore*—before; *lownsome*—calm; *dern intil't*—
hide inside it; *whiles*—occasionally; *kythes*—appears; *ayont*—beyond;
kittles up—stimulates; *spreit*—spirit; *gowden flouer*—golden flower.

SIC TRANSIT GLORIA MUNDI

*On viewing the remains of a clerical dignitary in a
medieval grave at Whithorn Priory.*

Aye, ye were a braw chiel aince!
Gowd ring on your fingur,
Jewelled cleik to hird your flock,
Nae dout a braw singer
When ye weet your whustle at the mass wi
Wine frae a siller-gilt tassie.
And look at ye nou!
Sax centuries, and the wecht
O sax fute o mools hae wrocht
A bonnie transformation
That hardly suits your station,
Crozier crookit and scruntit,
Chalice and paten duntit,
Hause-bane dwynit,
Harn-pan crynit,
Your chaft-blade ajee
Juist like a Campbell's,
But that couldna be!
In Candida Casa a Campbell
Has never held the see.

And thon chiel frae the Meenistry,
Thon archeological resurrectionist,
He'll meisure ye in your kist
And tak a likeness o ye
Wi infra-reid, or aiblins
Ultra-violet ye,
The scientists syne will get ye,
Wi gaga-coonter vet ye,
Jalousin what's your age.
In jaurs they'll catalyse ye,

Ettlin to analyse ye,
Sin that's nou aa the rage.

Syne when ye're tabulatit,
Recordit, and debatit,
And richtly written doun,
They'll set ye in a case
In thon Museum place
In Edinburgh Toun.
The folk that hear your fame
Will come on holiedays
And dress't in Sabbath claes
Mind ye on aulden days
And gar ye feel at hame.

aye—yes; *braw*—fine; *chiel*—fellow; *aince*—once; *cleik*—crook; *weet your whustle*—wet your whistle; *siller*—silver; *tassie*—cup; *mools*—the grave; *scruntit*—scratched; *duntit*—beaten; *hause-bane*—neck-bone; *dwynit*—wasted; *harn-pan*—skull; *crynit*—shrunken; *chaft-blade*—jaw-bone; *ajee*—awry; *Campbell*—crooked mouth; *kist*—chest; *aiblins*—perhaps; *jalousin*—guessing; *ettlin*—intending; *sin*—since; *aa*—all; *claes*—clothes; *gar*—make.

D. M. BLACK b. 1941

WITH DECORUM

I lay down and having
died, gave my instructions. They
filled the room with
balloons and streamers, cherubim at the four
corners of the ceiling blowing their bright bugles—
laid me on a carved catafalque, in an em-
broidered robe

27

crusted with emeralds; doctor and
priest in black mantles;
inconsolable women. Trundling of
wheels, the entire
building moves to the cemetery. Seagulls are
crying at the shut window. The ba-
lloons joggle.
    I sit up and bellow : Death,
then, it is
time for the
party!—we
draw decanters out of the coffin, tear in our
teeth the candy lilies; ah the
trumpets' Reveille, the
rollicking floor. Open the
windows, Jock! My
beauties, my
noble horses—yoked in
pairs, white horses, drawing my great
hearse, galloping and
frolicking over the cropped turf.

THE RED JUDGE

We shut the red judge in a bronze jar
—By 'we,' meaning myself and the black judge—
And there was peace, for a time. You can have enough
Yowling from certain justices. The jar
We buried (pitching and swelling like the tough
Membrane of an unshelled egg) on the Calton Hill.
And there was peace, for a time. My friend the black
Judge was keen on whisky, and I kept
Within earshot of sobriety only by drinking
Slow ciders, and pretending

Unfelt absorption in the repetitive beer-mats. It was a kind of
Vibration we noticed first—hard to tell
Whether we heard it or were shaken by it,
Whether the tumblers quivered or our minds. It grew
To a thick thudding, and an occasional creak
Like a nearby axle, but as it were
Without the sense of 'nearby'—The hard flag-
stones wriggled slightly under the taut linoleum.
I supported the black judge to the nearest door—
Detached his clutched glass for the protesting barman—
And propped him against a bus-stop. Maybe
It was only a pneumatic drill mating at Queen Street,
Or an impotent motor-bike—the sounds grew harsher:
My gestures stopped a 24 that spat
Some eleventh commandment out of its sober driver,
But I was more conscious of the rocking walls,
The pavement's shrugging off its granite kerb. . . .

Quite suddenly the night was still: the cracks
In the roadway rested, and the tenements
Of Rose Street stood inscrutable as always. The black judge
Snored at his post. And all around
The bright blood filled the gutters, overflowed
The window-sills and door-steps, soaked my anyway
Inadequate shoes, and there was a sound of cheering
Faintly and everywhere, and the Red Judge walked
O thirty feet high and scarlet towards our stop.

THE EDUCATORS

In their
limousines the
teachers come: by
hundreds. O the
square is

blackened with dark suits, with grave
scholastic faces. They
wait to be summoned.
                              These are the
educators, the
father-figures. O you could
warm with love for the firm lips, the
responsible foreheads. Their
ties are strongly set, between their collars. They
pass with dignity the exasperation of waiting.

A
bells rings. They turn. On the
wide steps my
dwarf is standing, both hands raised. He
cackles with laughter. Welcome, he cries, welcome,
to our elaborate Palace. It is indeed. He
is stumbling in cartwheels over the steps. The
teachers turn to each other their grave faces.

With
a single grab they have him up by the shoulders. They
dismantle him. Limbs, O
limbs and delicate organs, limbs and
guts, eyes, the tongue, the
lobes of the brain, glands; several tonsils,
eyes, limbs, the tongue,
a kidney, pants, livers, more
kidneys, limbs, the tongue
pass from hand to hand, in their serious hands. He is
utterly gone. Wide
crumbling steps.

They
return to their cars. They
drive off smoothly, without disorder;
watching the road.

30

That the fine paunch is a hostage to fortune I
took no telling. In my
own case I
always dieted and in the
passion of hunger chose rather to
chew wire than to succumb to the
lure of bread. Nevertheless de-
spite one's discipline one is made
vulnerable with every gesture! As I
waded the streets one burgeoning evening crying
out with pain I was
met by the Inspector of Circuses(!): in
high spurred boots and tailcoat, shouting: Are you
up to our Standard? (I was
biting into a stiff nest of wire.) Right!—I
shivered. He
cracked his kiboko. I
turned, but a
cage was
over my head: with a
ringing clang (a
ringing clang!) the
gate fell to the pavement. Cloth: and in
darkness I
felt my cage wander out in the air—
clatter onto a lorry that
roared briskly.

                                    In the precincts
we are well kept, and I find in my a-
ppalled presence buckets of
meat and bread. I
hurl them out but they
are brought back. How my
belly screams for that comfort. I

break at last : like a
man filling a blast-furnace. And at the
showing, how should I
put on my
Act? They whip me. Wilful
refusal of work! What use for my
gathering back and buttocks! they whip me and whip me. I
sob, sob, into my tangled wire.

ALAN BOLD b. 1943

CAUSE AND EFFECT

He thought before the war
Of conflicts, heroisms, enemies
Who had to be crushed;
Causes that had to be fought for.

He had no time before the war
For bright skies, fields, the warm
Sun, his woman—only
Causes that had to be fought for.

I see him now after the war
In my lifetime. I notice his love
Of the sun, bright skies, fields, his woman :
Causes that have to be fought for.

THE POINT OF LOVE

What does it mean to be born?
Only a few substantial flips around the sun?
Only dependence on one star in infinity?
Only a second in a larger century?
Only a fraction of the omnipotent One?

Or the instigation of a passionate affair.
Or the reason for the beauty of her hair.
Or the centre of her particular universe.
Or the one that makes our death seem less fierce.
Or the deadly enemy of her despair.

But what if she is only human flesh
Destined to decay, to fly only to crash?
Only one in millions, a pointless whim
Of fate, a trick of carbon, an evanescent flame?
A remnant of the sentiment we have to smash?

Or the very point of staying alive
In a place so viciously combative.
Or the stimulation of the brain
Or the one who makes your life your own again
Or the entity that in herself defines love.

THE END

The world is almost dead. The last smile
Has flickered from the last face.
The sun scatters light over this heap
And the spinning earth crashes into night.
From distances too great ever to be thought

33

Nothing changes. No one sighs. Nothing breaks,
Though countless suns shine on and age.
We were a people aching for experience
And dying from it too. Now it is accomplished.
Perhaps not yet in fact, but certainly
In principle; and all the meretricious junk
That constitutes our life cannot disguise the end.
It was strange to go through birth to learn
To despise death and then later to concede it.
Can you remember? How the sensory ecstasy
Of growing glorified everything extraneous?
That fish that glistened only for your hook,
Those birds that seemed to fly for you, flowers
Reserving their minor miracles complete in every sense,
Animals panting at your touch, vegetation caressing
You? It was the same for me.
But something happened to change that, to change
Our world into a segment of a fragment,
And happiness became the thing we knew
Could never last. And so the moon, the sun
No longer mattered but became
Undistinguished lights. Ugly because seen
By no one. What is special apart from life?
And that is gone. Do I anticipate?
Perhaps in time, but time is happening.
This time we're all in it together.
And then I'll tell you, I'll be able to,
How I loved you all, how my faults
Were only faked, how I appreciated every one
Of you. There won't be time unless I say it now
But there's a taste that holds me back
You understand. That's all I have to say.

SIX DIMENSIONS

We move in five dimensions you must know:
First, revolving; second, orbiting the sun;
Third, tied to the sun in unearthly slow
Galactic revolutions; fourth, the one

That splits astronomers, our rapid flight
From other galaxies; and fifth, the way
We walk about on earth—the speed of light
Not being in our picture of the day.

But I believe there is another trace
Of movement that has some significance
To our minute position in all space:

This is a moving dependent on chance.
It is the way a look, a touch, can give
An absolute necessity to live.

THE TWO CULTURES

The Trifid Nebula to my green eyes
Looks like an aged pundit gazing down
At worlds of mortals; I see a frown
And tilted head and folded hands; a wise

Old meditating gentleman who tries
To do his best but gets weary. A crown
Of stars suspended to his left; a gown
Of white silk wrapped round him. He nods and sighs.

I know I see like this because I use

A heritage of seeing to direct
All shapes into a schematic pattern.

I know that man's great task is to unlearn
These modes of seeing, that he must expect
The unexpected. But what does he lose?

From   EDINBURGH CASTLE

As if a few odd bombs were bouncing round
The globe, the third world war engulfed us all.
That day many people walked the streets as they had
For ten or twenty years, or perhaps more.
The buses kept on moving and the roads
Though hardly perfect had just done so far.
Out on some remote island in the East
The thing had gone too far; the brink was brinked
And then the guts of cities spewed their load.
We could only wait. Other places,
So we heard, were ripped apart, and flames
Were seen for miles. All the pipes, the tubes
That carry power underneath a town
Were gone. All was just one tangled mesh
Of wire, rock, rubble and some human bones.
This is what we heard, but our means
Of communication were faltering.

Fingers scraped in cities far away
From underneath a tomb of rotten earth
(Where plants no longer photosynthesise).
The flesh that melted from the bones like wax
Melting from an iron armature
Gave us reason to be lucky *here*.
We had been missed out in the capitals

The two sides thought of as strategic points
And so—we had the world to ourselves!

THE REALM OF TOUCHING

Between my lips the taste of night-time blends
And then dissolves. It is blank as my eyelids close.
For a flickering of time I concentrate on how time ends.

It should be present, the scent of the rose
We bought, though one petal has begun to fall.
Somehow that simplifies the girl I chose.

Night music must be the sweetest sound of all.
It is made to overwhelm with virtuosity.
But every night it is the same pounding on the same wall.

Nocturnal images are said to be the ones that stay
Longest, with exploitation of the dark half-tone.
This I disregard and watch for the day.

A touch in the realm of touching alone
Adds presence to the absence of light.
A clasp of hands, then bodies, my own
And hers is when I welcome the blindness of night.

GEORGE MACKAY BROWN b. 1921

IKEY ON THE PEOPLE OF HELLYA

Rognvald who stalks round Corse with his stick
I do not love.

His dog has a loud sharp mouth.
The wood of his door is very hard.
Once, tangled in his barbed wire
(I was paying respects to his hens, stroking a wing)
He laid his stick on me.
That was out of a hard forest also.

Mansie at Quoy is a biddable man.
Ask for water, he gives you rum.
I strip his scarecrow April by April.
Ask for a scattering of straw in his byre
He lays you down
Under a quilt as long and light as heaven.
Then only his raging woman spoils our peace.

Gray the fisherman is no trouble now
Who quoted me the vagrancy laws
In a voice slippery as seaweed under the kirkyard.
I rigged his boat with seven curses.
Occasionally still, for encouragement,
I put the knife in his net.

Though she has black peats and a yellow hill
And fifty silken cattle
I do not go near Merran and her cats.
Rather break a crust on a tombstone.
Her great-great-grandmother
Wore the red coat at Gallowsha.

The thousand rabbits of Hollandsay
Keep Simpson's corn short,
Whereby comes much cruelty, gas and gunshot.
Tonight I have lit a small fire.
I have stained my knife red.
I have peeled a round turnip.
And I pray the Lord
To preserve those nine hundred and ninety nine innocents.

Finally in Folscroft lives Jeems,
Tailor and undertaker, a crosser of limbs,
One tape for the living and the dead.
He brings a needle to my rags in winter,
And he guards, against my stillness
The seven white boards
I got from the Danish wreck one winter.

WEDDING

With a great working of elbows
The fiddlers ranted
  —*Joy to Ingrid and Magnus!*

With much boasting and burning
The whisky circled
  —*Wealth to Ingrid and Magnus!*

With deep clearings of the throat
The minister intoned
  —*Thirdly, Ingrid and Magnus.*

Ingrid and Magnus stared together
When midnight struck
At a white unbroken bed.

JESS OF THE SHORE

The three fishermen said to Jess of the Shore
"A wave took Jock

39

Between the Kist and the Sneuk.
We didn't get him. We wouldn't give much for his life."
They left Jock's share of fish at the door.
She laid off the gray shawl.
She put on the black.
She took the score of shrugging fish
And a sharp knife
And went the hundred steps to the rock,
A cold wife
In a cold measured ivory ritual.

COUNTRY GIRL

I make seven circles, my love
For your good breaking.
I make the gray circle of bread
And the circle of ale
And I drive the butter round in a golden ring
And I dance when you fiddle
And I turn my face with the turning sun till your
    feet come in from the field.
My lamp throws a circle of light,
Then you lie for an hour in the hot unbroken
    circle of my arms.

FARM LABOURER

"God, am I not dead yet?" said Ward, his ear
    Meeting another dawn.
      A blackbird, lost in leaves, began to throb
And on the pier

The gulls stretched barbarous throats
Over the creels, the haddock lines, the boats.
His mortal pain
All day hung tangled in that lyrical web.

"Seventy years I've had of this," said Ward,
   "Going in winter dark
      To feed the horse, a lantern in my fist,
Snow in my beard,
         Then thesh in the long barn
         Bread and ale out of the skinflint corn,
      And such-like work!"
         And a lark flashed its needle down the west.

COUGH CURE

All Monday he sat by the fire, Stoney the fisherman
Loud with the hoast,
Till Jean bought bronchial mixture from the van.
In terror at the black stuff in the bottle,
When Jean was out, luring an egg from the hen,
He coughed his way to the roust
And launched the *Belle* with a roll and a rattle
Into a sea
Shaken with spasms as loud and green as he.
He came back at night
With a score of lobsters, sillocks like stars, a skate
As wide and bright as the moon
And devil a hoast.
"Stoney, this day thy creels and hooks lay well. . . ."
But there, a patient Penelope on the coast
Stood Jean with a spoon
And a long bottle, seething and black as hell!

THE YEAR OF THE WHALE

The old go, one by one, like guttered flames.
  This past winter
    Tammag the bee-man has taken his cold blank mask
    To the honeycomb under the hill,
      Corston who ploughed out the moor
    Unyoked and gone; and I ask,
  Is Heddle lame, that in youth could dance and saunter
      A way to the chastest bed?
The kirkyard is full of their names
      Chiselled in stone. Only myself and Yule
        In the ale-house now, speak of the great whale year.

This one and that provoked the taurine waves
  With an arrogant pass,
    Or probing deep through the snow-burdened hill
    Resurrected his flock,
      Or passed from fiddles to ditch
    By way of the quart and the gill,
  All night lay tranced with corn, but stirred to face
      The brutal stations of bread;
While those who tended their lives
    Like sacred lamps, chary of oil and wick,
      Died in the fury of one careless match.

Off Scabra Head the lookout sighted a school
  At the first light.
    A meagre year it was, limpits and crows
    And brief mottled grain.
      Everything that could float
    Circled the school. Ploughs
Wounded those wallowing lumps of thunder and night.
      The women crouched and prayed.
Then whale by whale by whale
    Blundering on the rock with its red stain
      Crammed our winter cupboards with oil and meat.

LOVE LETTER

To Mistress Madeline Leslie, widow
At Quoy, parish of Voes, in the time of hay:

The old woman sat in her chair, mouth agape
At the end of April.
There were buttercups in a jar at the window.

The floor is not blue now
And the table has flies and bits of crust on it.
Also the lamp glass is broken.

I have the shop at the end of the house
With sugar, tea, tobacco, paraffin
And, for whisperers, a cup of whisky.

There is a cow, a lady of butter, in the long silk grass
And seven sheep on Moorfea.

The croft girls are too young.
Nothing but giggles, lipstick, and gramophone records.

Walk over the hill Friday evening.
Enter without knocking
If you see one red rose in the window.

BUTTER

Where has my butter gone? The
vanman, he took seven pounds
and a basket of warm eggs, for
jam, sugar, tea, paraffin. I
gave the tinkers a lump, to keep
this away, the black word from our
byre. I put some in the damp peats,
to coax a flame. I swear the cat
has a yellow tongue. There was only
a scrape for the fisherman's bannock
like a bit of sun on a dull day. The
old cow is giving me a mad look.

HADDOCK FISHERMEN

Midnight. The wind yawing nor-east.
A low blunt moon.
Unquiet beside quiet wives we rest.

A spit of rain and a gull
In the open door.
The lit fire. A quick mouthful of ale.

We push the *Merle* at a sea of cold flame.
The oars drip honey.
Hook by hook uncoils under The Kame.

Our line breaks the trek of sudden thousands.
Twelve nobbled jaws,
Gray cowls, gape in our hands.

44

Twelve cold mouths scream without sound.
The sea is empty again.
Like tinkers the bright ones endlessly shift their ground.

We probe emptiness all the afternoon,
Then pause and fill our teeth
With dependable food, beef and barley scone.

Sunset drags its butcher blade
From the day's throat.
We turn through an ebb salt and sticky as blood.

More stars than fish. Women, cats, a gull
Mewl at the rock.
The valley divides the meagre miracle.

HAMNAVOE MARKET

They drove to the Market with ringing pockets.

Folster found a girl
Who put wounds on his face and throat,
Small and diagonal, like red doves.

Johnston stood beside the barrel.
All day he stood there.
He woke in a ditch, his mouth full of ashes.

Grieve bought a balloon and a goldfish.
He swung through the air,
He fired shotguns, rolled pennies, ate sweet fog from a stick.

Heddle was at the Market also.
I know nothing of his activities.
He is and always was a quiet man.

Garson fought three rounds with a negro boxer,
And received thirty shillings,
Much applause, and an eye loaded with thunder.

Where did they find Flett?
They found him in a brazen circle,
All flame and blood, a new Salvationist.

A gypsy saw in the hand of Halcro
Great strolling herds, harvests, a proud woman.
He wintered in the poorhouse.

They drove home from the Market under the stars
Except for Johnston
Who lay in a ditch, his mouth full of dying fires.

DEAD FIRES

At Burnmouth the door hangs from a broken hinge
And the fire is out.

The window at Shore empty sockets
And the hearth coldness.

At Bunnerton the small drains are choked.
Thrushes sing in the chimney.

Stars shine through the roofbeams of Scar.
No flame is needed
To warm ghosts and nettles and rats.

Greenhill is sunk in a new bog.
No kneeling woman
Blows red wind through squares of ancient bog.

The Moss is a tumble of stones.
That black stone
Is the stone where the hearth-fire was rooted.

And in Midhouse among those flowers of flame
Bread and fish were baked.
That enchanted stone turned the blue lobster red.

In Crowsnest the sunken hearth
Was an altar for priests of legend.
Old seamen from the clippers with silken beards.

The three-toed pot at the wall of Park
Is lost to women's cunning.
A slow fire of rust eats the cold iron.

The sheep drift through Reuming all winter.
Sheep and snow
Blanch fleetingly the black stone.

It is still there,
The flat stone in Windbrake where the water-pot stood,
But always the eye looks for the charred stone.

From the sacred stone the children of the valley
Drifted lovewards
And out of labour to the lettered stone in the kirkyard.

The fire beat like a heart in each house
From the first corner-stone
Till they led through a sagging lintel the last old ones.

The poor and the good fires are all quenched.
Now, cold angel, keep the valley
From the bedlam and cinders of a Black Pentecost.

LAOTIAN PEASANT SHOT
(seen on television war report documentary)

He ran in the living air,
Exultation in his heels.

A gust of wind will erect
A twisting tower of dried leaves
That will collapse when
The breath is withdrawn.

He turned momentarily,
His eyes looking into his fear,
Seeking himself.

When he fell the dust
Hung in the air
Like an empty container
Of him.

THE RED SKY

Till that moment the church spire
At the top of our street was encased
In that blue sky. Occasionally white
Puffclouds drove straight to heaven.
At the foot of our street
The Central Public School, granite,
Also encased in blue.
We lived between with the
Worms, forkies, shell-fish, crabs—

All things that crept from stones,
And with the daisies for company.

Each was alive and very worthy,
Just right, till I met
The curly boy with square shoulders
Who knocked me down
Pushing his fist into my teeth.
Then a crack ran through the red sky.
From then on it was never the same.

FIRE AND EARTH

My attic window sights roof-topped
horizons with one gold autumn tree,
its branched candelabra lit
by quick-fire contained by earth's lid,
translated to finger tips of tree,
leaf trembling in a slight wind.
Somewhere within, the sap drives
upwards—like a flame held
in a lamp-glass drawn by the funnel—
chancing the setting bone of winter.
Somewhere a concealed bird sings.

O but this boldness is dashed,
put aside by the thin, city mist,
whitening, flattening till tree
is delicate as a Chinese painting.
Without dimension, this world is quality;
like the air of a tune remembered
precisely, but long after singing.

From VISITATIONS FROM A WAR-TIME CHILDHOOD

I.

Of the five waiters, white, stiff-shirt fronted
With silver trays on the tips of fingers,
At the ready with napkins as white
As their paper faces,
Four were perfect.

The fifth had a shoe-lace untied.
His waxwork tear at his eye
Registered discomfiture,
Conveyed his regret to the single customer
In the corner.

The naphthalene lighting placed the scene;
Edwardian. One
Should not shop at this restaurant
Longer than need be
But pass on to carnage.

II.

1914.
He returned in 1917,
His legs bandaged in khaki,
His boots shining new polished.
Marvellous how he had got rid of the trenches.

The only reminder
Was the thin red line at this throat.

50

III.

Now when big-brother Arthur
Stepped
Over our granite doorstep
With his soldier's Balmoral
In his hand

And we had shut the door
On the bright sea
That customarily roared
Outside
And he stood there waiting

For the mother to say
"You're home and no different."
And the jolly father
To say
"How many Boche this time?"

I put up my finger
To touch the warm flesh
Of the hero who had
Actually killed
A man

And in a good cause.

But there was no difference
In that hand.

PIGEON'S FEATHER BY SAINTE CHAPELLE, PARIS

These skies have never quite emptied
of angels.

      Tack teeth smiling pin-tables,
      nickel spinning miles of
      battering fruit machines, op
      pop, cliff-top in plush tip-ups,
      wrapped goods—is O.K. for a
      smart polish in a close neon night

but these skies have never quite emptied
of angels.

      Out of that pale blue
      Angelico in the Louvre
      down by Sainte Chapelle
      a white feather
                  floated.

      Peace,
      "nostra pace"
      maybe
      was somewhere around.

THE SINGERS

O Thalassa! Thalassa! Where, where
Are the winged instruments of celebration?
Where are singers of today?
We did not know that our sea, debauched
By old men's pilferings, sullied by paddling boys,

Was not unsimilar to Homer's ocean,
Our bitter, treacherous coast reminiscent.
We did not know the music of the Ancient World
Whispered with the spindrift at our back door,
Offered its strange acclamation with wintry thunderings
For all who would hear. But we
Would not, could not, had no eyes for the dawn,
No ears for the wavering music of the wind.

> The porridge pot is on the fire,
> The spelding 's frae the rack,
> Or we can catch the tide at five
> Ower meat we maun be swack.

> Charlie 's at the pier lang syne
> Tae fuel engine and test her.
> Hist ye, Meg, the baited lines
> And hist ye, lass, ma s'wester.

And the music was there waiting—years back—
For the singers of love and violence
To tell the tale at the roaring night-fire
Into the unborn future.

> Drap the anchor Charlie! Dod,
> We're tee the gruns noo,
> If but the weather 'll only haud
> We'll full the boxes foo.

> But gin she blaw anither bittock
> Or shift a pint tae north
> Nae one whiting, cod or haddock,
> Nae a maik we're worth.

Songs—in a land of the strange and the common—
The irregular crags in the green winter light,
The frozen fall in the secret corrie,

The caves with the sounding waters,
The caves of the dying birds,
The hollow hills and the deadly currents
And the slow sun rising on the ordinary landscape.
The country of low stone dykes and tractable fields,
The man at his labour in the field,
The obedient dog, the sheep on the low hill,
The woman at the baking board,
The children with blue butterflies in the hard sun
On the road to the shore.
A boy with a can of milk walks to the shore,
Returns with shining herring to the dark land.

> Throttle her doon, Dod,
> At thon black rock,
> Tide 's running strang, Dod,
> We'll coup gin she knock.

> A sair tyave it wis, boy,
> In yon black swell,
> But we're hame wi' a shot, boy,
> Will dee us well.

In the cold morning as day
Stretches on the hills—the beginning,
The resumption of the tasks of the day,
The woman moving about the house,
The child crying, the cattle heaving
In their stalls. The boat goes from the pier,
The wind creeps to the wide waterways,
The ploughman drives the long furrow,
And in the prime of day—activity.
By the road to the shore in the sun
The sheep's backs are dappled with sweetness.
Happiness spreads like summer.
At night the world is in the mouths of men
Till the flames are down and the embers ash.

Lat go that rope, loon,
Watch, she'll brak.
Smert 's the word, loon,
Or she snap.

Alec John's deid.
Ae weet nicht
Slipped, cracked his heid,
Pitten oot in sma licht.

Our coasts have no laurels—only the white dawn.
Yesterday the seas cavorted, brought
With the thin spume, Alec John's blue mitt.
Yesterday a fankled line took Sandy,
A pot in the wrinkled sand foundered Jack Bayne.
To salvage *The Water Lily* was a fikey business—
The crew were all young men.
We did not know as the tides came upon us
And our river ran in spate to the sea
Our waters were touched by the Athenian sun.

Where, where are the singers,
Where the winged instruments of celebration?

spelding—salted fish; *ower*—over; *swack*—active; *lang syne*—long ago;
hist ye—hasten; *tee*—to, at; *gruns*—fishing-grounds; *foo*—full; *gin*—if;
bittock—little bit; *maik*—halfpenny; *coup*—upset; *tyave*—struggle; *loon*
lad; *pitten*—put; *fikey*—troublesome.

TOM BUCHAN b. 1931

THE WEEK-END NATURALIST

My humanoid friend, myself, a limited animal

55

in love with the planet
escaping across the dumb topographies of Assynt
with maps and a compass
taking incorrect fixes on anonymous Bens
staring into bog-pools

entertaining myself with half-formulated notions
of a non-utilitarian character
and applying my ragbag of ecological data
to flowers which I recognise
absentmindedly as if they were old friends
whose names I've forgotten

timidly leaping backwards at the green skeleton
of a ewe
scared out of my wits by an equally terrified stag
and always very much conscious
of my wet socks, my deaf ear, balding pate
and over-filled gut

but retaining even here persistent after-images
of my bank-balance
the impersonal malevolence of ill-paid officials
the pretensions
of well-paid academics, the dishonesties of shopkeepers
car-salesmen and politicians

until my vague fountain of speculative ideas
coalesces into irritability
and these innocent towers of darkening gneiss
stand over me
like tax inspectors as I trip on a delinquent peat
and fall on my face.

THE FLAMING MAN

The flaming man who slowly
in slow motion slowly runs and falls
slowly over backwards in slow motion burning
with his eyes wide open in his dream of pain

is concentrating
is preoccupied with shaking off his dream
of burning but falls over backwards slowly
burning falls over slowly backwards burning

trying to put his flames out by rolling
in the brittle grass beside the hut
from which a curious child looks calmly out
at the camera which steadies its distorting lens

upon the burning man who tries to rise
upon one elbow from his couch of burning napalm
and takes deep slow-motion intakes of incredible air
to bear the fire with which he's burning

skin burns flesh burns bones burn
fat burns nerves burn brain burns
the world 's on fire for him
but he is calm

slowly awakening from his dream of fire
his face is calm
as he lies down in napalm like the phoenix
and burns.

DOLPHINS AT COCHIN

They crashed among the spider-nets
spluttering and breathing hoarsely
chasing fish out of the water,
calling one another and disappearing.

Lime-green bellies and smiling mouths
sliced upwards obliquely,
calm humorous eyes regarded us for a moment
and splashed back.

Sea-marks of dolphins moved
among the dozens of jockeying sails,
a mile out in the breaking waves
we could see the flash of more dolphins.

On the bridge of our tanker the grey paint
blistered in the heat; above us
the siren mooed to come in at the jetty,
the water green and translucent.

The smell of crude oil, of ginger
drying in the yards; piles of coloured fish;
the creak of a wooden capstan,
monkeys quarrelling on top of the parked cars.

And suddenly there was a dolphin inside
our slow bow-wave—revolving, amused,
not realising our incomprehension
of his vivid thoughts.

Two dolphins came skidding round the point,
screeched to a standstill
blowing vapour and circling each other;
then they raced on again, leaping.

From our primitive element
we watched them helplessly
able only to think of cold metaphors
or to anthropomorphize.

But they wheeled: dolphins!
their liquid backs, their arched fins
moving steadily out from the shore
into the hilarious ocean.

THE LOW ROAD

Bohannan held onto a birch branch
by yon bonny banks and looked down
through several strata of liquid
—there is someone somewhere
aiming a missile at me (he thought)
for the mountain behind him
was drilled with caves
each one crammed with nuclear hardware
and the sea-loch over the mountain
lay easy with obsolescent new submarines.

Would an underwater burst at Faslane
kill me (Walter Bohannan)
and for how many seconds/split seconds
would its bubble of steam swell and rupture
and swell and rupture again as it rose
to its final spiflication
sending fission products skimming
across the surface to Rhu and Roseneath
and Garelochhead and Greenock and Rothesay?

But no doubt they'll have arranged
for an airburst over Glen Douglas
the fireball of which will deforest Inchlonaig,
vaporize Cailness and Rowchoish, fry
the Glasgow councillors fishing for free
on Loch Katrine and kill all the spiders
and earwigs between here and Crianlarich
and me (he thought) as through the soft air
trucks, cars, buses and articulated lorries
accelerated their loads of Omo, people and bricks
towards Oban and Iveraray.

STEWART CONN b. 1936

THE ORCHARD

Loose-rigged, the orchard pitches
Like a sailing-ship caught on the swell
Of slapdash southern seas. Cargoes burst
In the hold, under canvas or barrel

On barrel piled high. And the sun
Is the colour of straw; and the sky,
Yanked brutally in, leaves heaps
Of apples rotting where they lie.

A drugged light swills the poop. Trees,
Mast and yard-arm, take the strain.
Air's bruised. Rain litters the yellow
Deck, then swabs it clear again.

Crushed branch, made flashing bowsprit,
Slithers under. Mashed shapes shoot

Through spindrift. Crude as Caliban,
Pigs stuff their filthy bellies and root

For more. Yet I remember
A simpler order in this place:
When boys in azure tunics climbed
Flimsy ladders and stepped out into space.

FLIGHT

Leaving the town behind, and the spoiled
    Fields, we made slowly for the hills.
        Our clothes were in rags, our
      Bodies lit with sores. Every
So often we had to water the horse.

Our farm-cart was heaped with straw. Under
        That, the real cargo.
      The soldiers scoffed. After
Searching us, though, they let us through.

We dared not stop, or look round.
    But from the side of the cart
      Came a steady trickle of blood
    Where the most drunken of the guards
Had run his sword in among the straw.

THE FOX IN HIS LAIR

The fox in his lair
by oak-root and whorl
is presence, not scent
of fox. Is cold fury
of fur—soft pad
of cunning by night.

The badger in his burrow
no fairy-tale brock,
but paw crooked like a nut
ready to tear
the earth's skin
to get at the bone.

The raven, sweeping
in air, no line
on a blue plate: but
gorger of carrion, meat
in his gullet, slivers
trailing from each talon.

And you, my sweet,
how can you hope
to convince me
you are all sweetness—
when I know where
your hands have burrowed?

Like badger, like raven
and fox, who inhabit
domains of their own
in air, you are
no mere colour or scent;
but of the earth, your rotten lair.

THE STORM

The horses stamping, the stable doors banging,
The storm-lanterns clanging and clanging,
I hunched under the blankets with my book
Listening to the weather strike. Shutting out
Everything but the pictures on the page :
Knights in doublets and greaves, thighs
Thonged, hauberks richly wrapped, gloves
Glinting, spurs flashing, swords at their sides;
Ladies sighing, moon-faced minstrels singing.

Until the roar outside was so great
I could no longer concentrate on the courtly
Slaying of giants; but crept to the window
To look out. It was as though something huge
Had broken from its tether, and was lashing
At man and beast. Shapes were clubbed from trees,
Bringing their riders crashing. Or came
Thundering from their stirrups to the ground.
Everything I heard was like the breaking of bones.

Then something in the sky snapped. The raiders,
Renewing their efforts, came again. The last
I saw was a group of men with black buskins
And billhooks, opening bellies, fighting
For a grip, thrusting in at the bowels.
Next morning the storm had blown itself out.
My book lay open on the bed. Outside
Was a heifer that had run loose overnight
And impaled itself on an iron stanchion.

THE KING

They scoured me and laid me
On two boards, supported by trestles.
The head facing east, arms crossed.
Then they lowered me
Into place, lighting candles
Before sealing the mouth of the cave.

My hair tied to an oak beam;
The rest of my body
Enveloped in hazel leaves.
On the walls, like tapestries,
The pelts of hounds—heads
Hinged, jaws grinning.

And alongside, the two youngest
Of my wives, breasts bared,
Gashes in their throats.
Already the air filches
Them, wrist and ankle
Contained by a green flame.

At my side, pitchers of wine
And water, trays of sweetmeats,
Barrels of honey and lard.
And my broadsword polished
So that it dazzles, the haft
Within easy reach of my fist.

These apart I have cushions
For comfort, silver coins,
Scrolls for a long hour, a horn
To waken the dead. But
I lie here, my skull still split.
So far, nothing has happened.

AYRSHIRE FARM

Every new year's morning the farmers
Would meet at "Harelaw" with their guns
For the shoot. Mungo red in the face,
Matthew hale as a tree, John huge
In old leather. The others in dribs
And drabs, shotguns over their shoulders,
Bags flopping at their sides, collars up.

We'd set out across the north park,
The glaur on our leggings freezing
As we left the shelter of the knowes.
No dogs. Even the ferrets on this day
Of days were left squealing behind
Their wire. We'd fan out, taking
The slope at a steady tramp.

Mungo always aimed first, blasting away
At nothing. Hugh cursed under his breath;
The rest of us kept going. Suddenly
The hares would rise from the bracken-clumps
And go looping downhill. I remember
The banks alive with scuts, the dead
Gorse-tufts splattered with shot.

One by one the haversacks filled,
The blood dripping from them, staining
The snow. Matthew still in front,
Directing the others; the sun red
Behind its dyke, the wind rising.
And myself bringing up the rear,
Pretending I was lost, become the quarry.

Three blasts on a whistle, the second
Time round. And, in from the sleet,

We would settle on bales with bottles
And flasks, to divide the spoils. The bodies
Slit, and hung on hooks to drip. The dogs
Scrabbling on their chains, Todd's stallion

Rearing at the reek of blood. Then in
To the fire and a roaring new year:
Old Martha and Mima scuffling to and fro,
Our men's bellies filling, hands
Slowly thawing. And for me, off to bed,
A pig in the sheets, the oil lamp
Throwing shadows of rabbits on the wall.

*

Last winter I covered the same ground
On my own, no gun. Old Martha and Mima
Have gone to rest. Todd has tethered
His horses under the hill. Mungo, too,
From a fall at the baling. Yet my breathing
Seemed to make their shapes; and Matthews's
And Hugh's, and my own bringing up the rear.

At the road-end I stopped and stood
For some time, just listening. My hands
Growing numb. Then I crossed the track
To where a single rabbit lay twitching,
Big-headed, eyes bulging, in pain.
I took the heaviest stone I could find;
And with one blow beat in its brains.

BLACK FRIDAY

Oot behind a lorry,
Peyin nae heed,
Ablow a doubledecker,
A poor wean deid.

Perra worn sannies,
Wee durrty knees,
Heh, erra polis,
Stand back please!

Lookit the conductriss,
Face as white as chalk,
Heh, see the driver but
Cannae even talk.

Anyone a witness?
Na, we niver saw,
Glad ah'm no the polis
Goin tae tell its maw.

Weemen windae-hingin,
Herts in their mooth,
It's no oor close, Lizzie
Oh Gawdstrewth!

Screams on the landin,
Twa closes doon,
It's no wee Hughie!
Poor Nellie Broon.

Phone up the shipyard,
Oh, what a shame!
Yes, we'll inform him,
Please repeat the name.

See Big Hughie,
Jokin wi the squad,
Better knock off, Heug,
Oh dear God.

Whit—no his laddie?
Aw, bloody hell!
D'ye see Hughie's face but,
He's just a boy himsel.

ablow—below; *wean*—child; *perra*—pair of; *sannies*—sandshoes; *erra
polis*—here's the police; *windae-hingin*—leaning from windows.

HELEN B. CRUICKSHANK b. 1886

PERADVENTURE
Genesis XVIII : 32

Peradventure
Era
Rut
Advent
Dare
Venture
Even
Need
Ten
Under
Read
End.

Note—The author had once hoped to found a literary magazine, to be
called *The Peradventure*, if ten just men could be found to finance it.
Alas!

FROM THE NIGHT-WINDOW

The night rattles with nightmares.
Children cry in the close-packed houses,
A man rots in his snoring.
On quiet feet, policemen test doors.
Footsteps become people under streetlamps.
Drunks return from parties,
Sounding of empty bottles and old songs.
The young women come home,
The pleasure in them deafens me.
They trot like small horses
And disappear into white beds
At the edge of the night.
All windows open, this hot night,
And the sleepless, smoking in the dark,
Making small red lights at their mouths,
Count the years of their marriages.

LANDSCAPE WITH ONE FIGURE

The shipyard cranes have come down again
To drink at the river, turning their long necks
And saying to their reflections on the Clyde,
"How noble we are."

The fields are waiting for them to come over.
The trees gesticulate into the rain,
The nerves of grasses quiver at their tips.
Come over and join us in the wet grass!

The wings of gulls in the distance wave
Like handkerchiefs after departing emigrants.
A tug sniffs up the river, looking like itself.
Waves fall from their small heights on river mud.

If I could sleep standing, I would wait here
Forever, become a landmark, something fixed
For tug crews or seabound passengers to point at,
An example of being a part of a place.

SHIPS

When a ship passes at night on the Clyde,
The swans in the reeds picking the oil from their feathers
Look up at the lights, the noise of new waves,
Against hill-climbing houses, malefic cranes.

A fine rain attaches itself to the ship like skin.
The lascars play poker, the Scottish mate looks
At the last lights, that one is Ayrshire,
Others on lonely rocks, or clubfooted peninsulas.

They leave restless boys without work in the river towns.
In their houses are fading pictures of fathers ringed
Among ships' complements in wartime, model destroyers,
Souvenirs from uncles deep in distant engine rooms.

Then the boys go out, down streets that look on water.
They say, "I could have gone with them,"
A thousand times to themselves in the glass cafés,
Over their American soft drinks, into their empty hands.

AUTUMNAL ELEGY

It is another autumn, the air closes
Around the large low moon with a blue constriction,
Round the reluctant leaf with a crisping hand.
The little winds make wispy crepitation.
The easy heat and rage are gone, the bland
Debility of summer. One supposes,
Poised on the downward slope of hesitation,
The thunder and the sweat are both a fiction:
Though housefronts shone with paint and shops with roses.

Around the large low moon with a blue constriction
The poet pulls his scarf of commonplaces,
Of luckless love and chilly assignation,
Too wrapped in thought against the cold to care
Though native woodnotes spiral to inflation
Or how her light is dimmed by his depiction
Of that one eye with its albino glare.
For all the phrases are like old friends' faces
As dull as a no-more-explored addiction.

The poet pulls his scarf of commonplaces
Around his chilly fate. All art is hollow;
These are the words that moved us long ago
And now like smiles through smoke in public-houses
Can reassure us of a warmth we know.
We seek the moment where it left its traces.
Some cry, beneath the moon's mask sleeping, rouses
The hounds to bay again, the hunt to follow,
And Actaeon to show his ghostly paces.

Around his chilly fate, all art is hollow
Like the long street with intermittences
Of light, such eyes, upon its dark façades.
The dogs are round him in the empty air.
This is the truth imagination adds
To smoke, to chatter, to the beer we swallow,
To conversations broken on the stair.
Our death is fed to us in magic pittances:
All these blank walls are faces of Apollo.

Like the long street with intermittences
Of light, our life. These autumn evenings move us
With beckoning windows, like the lamps of port:
The lives of others, that seem safe and warm,
As our lives seem to their lives, by report.
If exiled souls could live on these remittances
From other exiles, and sleep out the storm,
The heavens might rumble but could not reprove us:
No debt would ever meet its day of quittances.

Of light, our life, these autumn evenings move us
To make some shining show, to help the others
Who move with trepidation through the dark,
Who lost the hope of harbour long ago,
And only hear the hounds of Acteon bark.
But are there Watchers still who hate and love us,
Is there one Light by which all lights burn low?
Or only wanderers like ourselves, our brothers?
O Glow, O Guide, enlighten and approve us!

To make some shining show, to help the others,
May be one more of our deciduous poses
Heaped in its corner by the tidy year
And rising now in aromatic sorrow.
We fear, and we have reason for our fear,
Since hope lies gasping and the fire smell smothers
All we can guess of perfumes of tomorrow,

Smoke of the tripod tickling our noses,
We wonder now if any Sybil bothers.

Maybe one more of our deciduous poses
Will spike with green the sullen avenue
And beak the buds to cry at desperation
The brief defiance of another spring.
Though souls are not a vegetable nation
But more like rocks that need a second Moses,
To these recurrent images they cling.
The year is spent, and we have spent our revenue.
It is another autumn, the bank closes.

ROBIN FULTON b. 1937

ESSENTIALS

a poem, they say, must be all muscle
like a man swimming

if it must be dressed, let it wear tools
like a man climbing, hoisting kit up with him

or maybe you know a poem (like a goddess)
from the grace it doesn't need to have but has

when you watch a stream you know it is a stream
not entirely from the moving muscle of water
but from the fineries of light it wears

IN MEMORIAM ALBERTO GIACOMETTI

the more you pare the fatter it becomes—
by which you meant I suppose that leanness
occupies its space exactly

you pressed matter to vanishing point
your fingers restlessly expunged
the most tenuous superfluity

there is a limit though which now you've passed,
not to be at all is an extreme,
for us your existences are large

massive between slender definitions

HOW TO SURVIVE

the right word in the right place
is—say—a waterdrop
to the naked eye it is clear and round
smear it out on a slide light it
magnify it and it really is
a vast world of interrelated life

consider fortunate noah
one thing he might have taken
along with his stud menagerie
was a specimen waterdrop
to demonstrate the true nature
of the murderous element he rode

A DISCOVERY

his acquaintance with her ended this way

as when

having lived in the village a whole year
assuming without once consulting a map
that the hill behind the village was a plain hill
behind which was a desert of plain hills
with gaelic names and unrewarding summits

but having once walked further than usual
stumbling wide-eyed upon a steep valley
staring at clear water
a long blue mile of it, he stands
breathing space as wide as a new ocean

his acquaintance with her ended and what began
seems already as lifelong as a hill

VIRTUOSO

spider on water, running on
what? pure horizontal plane
expanse without thickness or next to none?
and that other fellow on the sandy bed
his feet twirling in spider-time with yours
his blob of body keeping its exact distance
do you ever consult him? have you once
compared notes on the tenuous element
in which you perform, you with your acrobatics
and he with his monomaniac dumb-show?

you'd expect me to envy your prancing on
such mere next-to-nothingness
your weightless fol-de-rols on a skin of light,
water is sticky, I know that from books,
you know it when you break the skin and drown

ATTIC FINDS

from a thirty year old pile
he pulled the inner works of a toy engine
nailed to a slab of wood for a boyish experiment

it made him think of the stumpy carcase
which was all that was left of a dead stoat
after his nervous attempt to skin it neatly

another find (surely older)
was a transfer in a brittle envelope
he soaked it and gingerly peeled it out

a bright wet smile
a girl in primary colours with
too many ribbons and an overlong skirt

her hands said welcome
but as the wet skin dried and shrank
her smile was agony and she was grasping for help

A METICULOUS OBSERVER

he watched the old men straggle

down uncomfortable paths
that straggled too broke off
and for no reason took up again

he watched boys with almost pre-
hensile feet on high walls
where they risked their short lives
for reasons no-one else would appreciate

he watched girls with newly-shaped
bodies advertising themselves
without guile in the summery light
and without needing a reason to guide them

he turned away and pulled his door
shut in his windowless room
blinked until his eyes could see
the least measure of light for
the least measure of experience
he could with honesty classify and learn

REMOTE

though far it's not difficult to reach
twenty miles from a remote village
then a three-mile trudge on the moor
(it feels like climbing a steep hill that's on the level)

there are rancid pools and green soft-spots
and small sticky plants that eat flies,
on the slopes deer pause, cautiously
aware of the wooden creature crawling on the loch

it's not difficult to stay, passive

to the heathery wind and summer rain, curious
about the age of wiry bits of trees
preserved in peat banks the water is hollowing out

leaving such a place behind you
is another matter, into the northern dusk
you hump your stiff trout and stiff bones
and what you half believe is a wiser sense of time

you have also found a new prison for the mind
it is always open
you have bad dreams about the frantic rower
cruelly enclosed by the vast space he's in

CLEARING UP

it wasn't until he began to give them away
that he really noticed what they looked like
and now engrossed in their appearance
he forgot the purpose of tools
the music in records the words in books
and the years of earning it took to buy them

he found pleasure in compiling a thorough list
of furniture utensils papers clothes
the fact that he would never use them again
seemed less pressing than the need
not to omit a single item
whose absence could be wrongly interpreted

his ideas were less tangible
but when at last he got them laid out
he honestly recognised they were not his
some were public property

some were shabby some priceless
his own attempts to arrange them had jumbled them up

his feelings like a houseful of cats
were conveniently not there, he thought
when they come back and find the place gone
I daresay some will die
there can't be many of them left
with more than a few of their nine lives intact

his memories were the most difficult to remove
he plucked out armfuls of undergrowth
surprised at the toughness of old stems
and the brightness of secret flowers
he couldn't understand how
they could be so tangled and still live

at last it was done and all he had left
was his body, even that looked
like someone else he had never seen before
he watched another man's blood
travel marvellous miles of veins
and he envied that man's luck in having
such an unusual and ingenious possession

ROBERT GARIOCH b. 1909

DAY-TRIP

A bonny glen, yon, wi a green strath,
a burn, arable howes, and a muckle ben,
wi hens, kye, aits, bere, yowes,
a clachan, a wee howff wi aipen door,
smelling of beer on draught and bacon frying,
gey sonsy-lukan wemen here and there,

tow-heidit bairns doukan ablow the brig,
twa-thrie bodachs, bien, wi naethin adae
but blether awa, and bide till denner-time,
while a wud-feart pig, wi a voice like an auld wife,
scrauchs til the wrang gode, Help! Help!

strath—river valley; *burn*—stream; *howes*—hollows; *muckle ben*—great
peak; *kye*—cows; *aits*—oats; *bere*—barley; *yowes*—ewes; *clachan*—small
village; *wee howff*—little pub; *aipen*—open; *gey*—very; *sonsy*—healthy;
tow-heidit bairns—fair-haired children; *doukan*—bathing; *bodachs*—old
men; *bien*—comfortable; *blether*—talk idly; *wud-feart*—madly afraid;
scrauchs—screeches; *wrang gode*—wrong god.

I'M NEUTRAL

Last night in Scotland Street I met a man
that gruppit my lapel—a kinna foreign
cratur he seemed; he tellt me, There's a war on
atween the Lang-nebs and the Big-heid Clan.

I wasna fasht, I took him for a moron,
naething byordnar, but he said, Ye're wan
of thae lang-nebbit folk, and if I can,
I'm gaunnae pash ye doun and rype your sporran.

Says he, I'll get a medal for this job:
we're watchan ye, we ken fine what ye're at,
ye're with us or agin us, shut your gob.

He gied a clout that knockit aff my hat,
bawlan, A fecht! Come on, the Big-heid Mob!
Aweill, I caa'd him owre, and that was that.

gruppit—gripped; *kinna*—kind of; *cratur*—creature; *atween*—between;
Lang-nebs—Long-noses; *heid*—head; *fasht*—worried; *byordnar*—extra-
ordinary; *wan*—one; *thae*—those; *gaunnae*—going to; *pash*—smash; *rype*
—ransack; *gied*—gave; *fecht*—fight; *aweill*—ah well; *caa'd*—shoved; *owre*
—over.

DID YE SEE ME?

I'll tell ye of ane great occasioun:
I tuke pairt in a graund receptioun.
Ye cannae hae the least perceptioun
hou pleased I was to get the invitatioun

tae assist at ane dedicatioun.
And richtlie sae; frae its inceptioun
the hale ploy was my ain conceptioun;
I was asked to gie a dissertatioun.

The functioun was held in the aipen air,
a peety, that; the keelies of the toun,
a toozie lot, gat word of the affair.

We cudnae stop it: they jist gaithert roun
to mak sarcastic cracks and grin and stare.
I wisht I hadnae worn my M.A. goun.

ane—a; *tuke pairt*—took part; *cannae*—can't; *richtlie sae*—rightly so; *frae*
—from; *hale ploy*—whole frolic; *ain*—own; *gie*—give; *piety*—pity; *keelies*
—louts; *toozie*—untidy; *cudnae*—couldn't; *jist gaithert roun*—just
gathered round.

I WAS FAIR BEAT

I spent a nicht amang the cognoscenti,
a hie-brou clan, ilk wi a beard on him
like Mark Twain's miners, due to hae a trim,
their years on aiverage roun three-and-twenty.

Of poetry and music we had plenty,
owre muckle, but ye maun be in the swim :
Kurt Schwitter's Ur-sonata that gaes "Grimm
glimm gnimm bimmbimm," it fairly wad hae sent ye

daft, if ye'd been there; modern jazz wi juicy
snell wud-wind chords, three new anes, I heard say,
by thaim that kent, new, that is, sen Debussy.

Man, it was awfie. I wad raither hae
a serenata sung by randy pussy,
and what a time a reel of tape can play !

nicht—night; *hie-brou*—high-brow; *ilk*—each; *hae*—have; *owre muckle*—
too much; *maun*—must; *gaes*—goes; *snell*—bitter; *wud-wind*—woodwind;
thaim—them; *kent*—knew; *sen*—since; *awfie*—awful; *wad raither hae*—
would rather have; *randy*—lustful.

SISYPHUS

Bumpity doun in the corrie gaed whuddran the pitiless whun
    stane.
Sisyphus, pechan and sweitan, disjaskit, forfeuchan and broun'd-
    aff,
sat on the heather a hanlawhile, houpan the Boss didna spy him,
seean the terms of his contract includit nae mention of tea-breaks,
syne at the muckle big scunnersome boulder he trauchlit aince
    mair,
Ach, hou kenspeckle it was, that he ken'd ilka spreckle and
    blotch on't.
Heavan awa at its wecht, he manhaunnlit the bruitt up the brae-
    face,
takkan the easiest gait he had fand in a fudder of dour years,

82

hauddan awa frae the craigs had affrichtit him maist in his
    youth-heid,
feelan his years aa the same, he gaed cannily, tenty of slipped
    discs.
Eftir an hour and a quarter he warslit his wey to the brae's heid,
hystit his boulder richt up on the tap of the cairn—and it stude
    there!
streikit his length on the chuckie-stanes, houpan the Boss wadna
    spy him,
had a wee look at the scenery, feenisht a pie and a cheese-piece.
Whit was he thinkan about, that he jist gied the boulder a wee
    shove?
Bumpity doun in the corrie gaed whuddran the pitiless whun
    stane,
Sisyphus dodderan eftir it, shair of his cheque at the month's
    end.

corrie—mountain hollow; *gaed whuddran*—went rushing; *whun stane*—
whinstone; *pechan*—panting; *sweitan*—sweating; *disjaskit*—worn out;
forfeuchan—exhausted; *broun'd-aff*—browned-off; *hanlawhile*—short
time; *syne*—then; *scunnersome*—disgusting; *trauchlit*—struggled; *aince
mair*—once more; *kenspeckle*—well-known; *spreckle*—speckle; *on't*—on
it; *wecht*—weight; *bruitt*—brute; *brae*—slope; *gait*—way; *fand*—found;
fudder—large number; *dour*—hard; *craigs*—rocks; *affrichtit*—frightened;
maist—most; *gaed cannily*—went carefully; *tenty*—wary; *warslit*—
struggled; *streikit*—stretched; *chuckie-stanes*—pebblestones; *gied*—gave;
dodderan—toddling; *shair*—sure.

BRITHER WORM

I saw a lang worm snoove throu the space atween twa stanes,
pokan its heid, if it had ane, up throu a hole in the New Toun,
up throu a crack ye wad hardly hae seen in an area of stane,
unkenn'd upliftit tons of mason-wark piled on the soil,
wi causey-streets, biggit of granite setts, like blank waas flat on
    the grund,
plainstane pavements of Thurso slabs laid owre the stane-aircht
    cellars,

the area fifteen feet doun, wi weill-fittan flagstanes, Regency
   wark.
Nou, in my deedit stane-and-lime property awntert a nesh and
   perfect worm,
and I was abasit wi thochts of what was gaun-on ablow my feet,
that the feu'd and rentit grund was the soil of the Drumsheuch
   Forest,
and that life gaed on inunder the grund-waa-stane and had sent
   out a spy,
jalousan some Frien of the Worms had brocht a maist welcome
   shoure,
whan I on my side of the crust had teemit a pail of water,
meaning to gie the place a guid scrub-doun wi a stable-besom.
Sae a lang, saft, sappy and delicate pink and naukit cratur
neatly wan out frae atween thae weil-fittan chiselled, unnaitural
   stanes.
I watched and thocht lang of the wonders of Nature, and didna
   muve,
and thocht of the deeps of the soil, deeper nor the sea, and I
   made nae sound.
A rat raxt frae a crack atween twa stanes.
My hale body sheuk wi the grue.
It keekit at me, and was gane.

snoove—glide; unkenn'd—unknown; causey-streets—cobbled streets;
biggit—built; stane-aircht—stone-arched; awntert—adventured; nesh—
delicate; gaun-on—going on; grund-waa-stane—central stone; jalousan—
guessing; brocht—brought; shoure—shower; teemit—emptied; guid—
good; besom—broom; naukit—naked; nor—than; raxt—stretched; grue—
shudder; keekit—peeped.

From GARIOCH'S REPONE TIL GEORGE BUCHANAN

In kep and goun, the new M.A.,
wi burnisht harns in bricht array

frae aa the bukes he's read,
nou realises wi dismay
he's left it owre late in the day
      to learn anither tred.
What has he got that he can sell?
nae maitter tho he scrieve a fell
guid-gauan prose style, Ethel M. Dell
      he canna rival.
Poetic pouers may win him praise
but guarantee nae fowth of days
      for his survival.
A kep and goun—what dae they maitter?
A kep and bells wad suit him better.
He's jist an orra human cratur,
      yaup as a lous.
Tho he be latinate and greekit,
he kens that ilka yett is steekit
      but Moray Hous.
Nou see him in his college blazer;
the Muse luiks on; it maun amaze her
      to see his tricks,
like shandy in the Galloway Mazer
or Occam tyauvan wi his razor
      to chop-up sticks.
Afore his cless he staunds and talks
or scrieves awa wi colour'd chalks;
      nae mair by Helicon he walks,
      or e'en St Bernard's Well.
In clouds of blackbrod stour he's jowan
anent some aibstract plural noun,
while aa the time his hert is lowan
      in its wee private hell.
At nine a.m. she hears him blaw
his whustle, and lay doun the law
out in the pleygrund, whether snaw
      shoures doun, or Phoebus shines.
Wi muckle tyauve she sees him caa

chaos til order; raw by raw
he drills his bairns in mainner braw,
   weill covert-aff in lines.
They mairch til the assembly-haa
to sing a psalm and hear a saw
or maybe jist a threit or twa,
   as the heidmaister chuse.
Syne in his room she sees him faa
to wark; she hears him rant and jaw
and hoast and hawk and hum and haw,
blatter and blawp and bumm and blaw
and natter like a doitit craw,
teachan his bairns to count and draw
and chant gizinties and Bee-baw,
and read and spell nad aa and aa,
faur owre taen-up wi maitters smaa
   to mind him of the Muse.
Whan schule has skailt, he maun awa,
whaur? ye may speir—to some green shaw
to meditate a poem?—Na!
   His lowsan-time is faur
aheid: to organise fi'baw
   and plouter in the glaur.
Late in the day he hirples hame
wi bizzan heid, a wee-thing lame,
and indisjeesters in his wame,
   and that may cause nae wunner:
the break spells duty, jist the same . . .
   to supervise schule-denner.
Sae ilka week and month and year
his life is tined in endless steir,
grindan awa in second-gear
   gin teaching be his fate.
The Muse, wha doesna share her rule
wi sordid maisters, leaves the fule,
   sans merci, til his fate.

Lat onie young poetic chiel
that reads thae lines tak tent richt weill :

THINK TWICE, OR IT'S OWRE LATE !

kep—cap; *harns*—brains; *scrieve*—write; *fell*—very; *guid-gauan*—good-going; *fowth*—plenty; *orra*—odd; *yaup*—hungry; *ilka yett*—every gate; *steekit*—shut fast; *Moray House*—Edinburgh's teacher-training college; *tyauvan*—working hard; *stour*—dust; *jowan*—ringing; *anent*—concerning; *lowan*—flaming; *bairns*—children; *faa*—fall; *hoast*—cough; *doitit craw*—silly crow; *gizinties*—goes-into's (counting); *Bee-baw*—children's song; *owre taen-up*—too occupied; *schule*—school; *skailt*—dispersed; *speir*—ask; *shaw*—grove; *lowsan-time*—time to stop work; *fi'baw*—football; *plouter*—splash; *glaur*—mud; *hirples*—limps; *wee-thing*—little; *indisjees-ters*—indigestion; *wame*—stomach; *tined*—lost; *gin*—if; *chiel*—fellow; *tak tent*—take care.

FLORA GARRY b. 1900

VILLAGE MAGDALEN

Yon wis nivvir a wird to lichtlify;
"Hooer o' Babylon," bleed-jeelin, Bible
Wird o' pooer, stern, magic, tribal.
Deleeriet drunks wid lift it, fechtin mad,
Or halflins swicket b' some mim-moo'd jaad
An' hotterin i' their ain young hell;
Bit nae afore a bairn, nor tull a beast,
An' nae tull Bell.

She bade in a bothy doon Steenybrae Lane.
She'd a yard an' a stackie o' peats,
A rain-water bowie, a lang hippan-towie,
An' aye the aul coach an' the smarrach o' geets.

87

Hushelt intull a man's cassen waterproof cwyte
An' a pair o' hol't tackety beets,
An' humfin a pyockfu' o' tatties or meal,
Or a birn o' rozetty reets,

Skushlin ben the dutch-side, her milk flagon in han',
Dyl't-lookin an' worth i' the queets—
Michty, fa'd lie ben the bowster fae yon,
An' fa the earth faddert yon geets?

She wisna a' come, said some. Maybe. Could be.
She wis washin ae day at Burngrain
Wi' yon muckle maasie on. Burnie's wife scraichs:
"Lordsake, Bella, nae surely again."
An' says Bell, wi' a dour kin' o' thraa tull her moo,
A' the time timmerin on wi' the sheets:
"We canna jook fit lies afore's. It's jist Fate
At's geen me a' yon smarrach o' geets."

Pooerfu, barritchfu wirds hae thir time an' place.
Bit less preceesion fyles may meet the case
An' dee less ull.
Better a kin'ly gley gin a dirten glower.
Easier to cower.
Sae ca' her sleekit, saft, a throwder baggerel.
Bit hooer? Na, nae Bell.

---

hooer—whore; *bleed-jeelin*—blood-congealing; *deleeriet*—delirious; *half-lins*—adolescents; *swicket*—cheated; *mim-moo'd*—prim-mouthed; *jaad*—jade; *hotterin*—stewing; *ain*—own; *tull*—to; *bade*—lived; *bothy*—cottage; *Steenybrae*—Stonyhill; *yard*—garden; *bowie*—container; *hippan-towie*—rope for hanging children's hip-napkins; *aul coach*—old perambulator; *smarrach*—untidy heap; *geets*—children (sometimes illegitimate); *hushelt* —stowed slovenly; *cassen*—thrown aside; *cwyte*—coat; *hol't*—holed; *tackety beets*—nailed boots; *humfin*—heavily carrying; *pyockfu'*— bag-full; *tatties*—potatoes; *birn*—burden; *rozetty reets*—resinous roots; *skushlin*—shuffling; *ben*—within; *dutch*—ditch; *dyl't*—silly; *worth i' the queets*—weak in the ankles; *fa'd*—who would; *ben the bowster fae yon*—along the bolster from that; *faddert*—fathered; *a' come*—completely sane;

ae—one; *muckle maasie*—big dress; *scraichs*—screeches; *thraa*—twist; *timmerin*—working strenuously; *jook*—dodge; *geen*—given; *pooerfu*—powerful; *barritchfu*—concentrated; *fyles*—whiles; *dee*—do; *ull*—ill; *gley*—squint; *dirten glower*—dirty scowl; *cower*—get over; *sleekit*—sly; *throwder*—unmethodical; *baggerell*—idiot.

DUNCAN GLEN b. 1933

CEREMONIAL

On the gress ablow the big-hoose winnock
A ceremonial sicht awaits the Colonel's folk,
A broun streekit mous lies in the set
O' rigor mortis. The tail straucht, lang and pintin
Frae the booed extended legs wi their pink taes
　　　　Braw shapit
　　　　But turnit in.

Abune the broken wame the sma feet
Pint in fixed stride the paradin flee
On the set face. Soon the tail will drap,
The flees form a company,
And troop the bricht colours o life on daith
　　　　Up and down
　　　　That braw set table.

ablow—below; *big-hoose*—big house (mansion); *winnock*—window; *sicht*—sight; *streekit*—outstretched; *mous*—mouse; *straucht*—straight; *pintin*—pointing; *booed*—bowed; *braw*—finely; *abune*—above; *wame*—belly; *flee*—fly; *braw*—fine.

MY FAITHER

Staunin noo aside his braw bress-haunled coffin
I mind him fine aside the black shinin range

89

In his grey strippit trousers, galluses and nae collar
For the flannel shirt. My faither.

I ken him fine thae twenty and mair years ago
Wi his great bauchles and flet auld kep;
And in his pooch the spottit reid neepkin
For usin wi snuff. My faither.

And ben in the lobby abune the braw shoon and spats,
Aside the silk waistcoat and claw-haimmer jaicket
Wi its muckle oxter pooch, hung the lum hat.
They caa'd him Jock the Lum. My faither.

And noo staunin wi thae braw shinin haunles
See him and me baith laid oot in the best
Black suitin wi proper white all weel chosen.
And dinna ken him. *My father.*

---

staunin—standing;   *bress-haunled*—brass-handled;   *galluses*—braces;
bauchles—old shoes; *flet auld kep*—flat old cap; *pooch*—pocket; *muckle oxter*—big shoulder; *lum hat*—silk hat; *baith*—both; *dinna ken*—don't know.

ERIC GOLD b. 1927

EMPEDOCLES IN PRINCES STREET

Dunedin—Edinburgh—Dunburgh.
A gey done burgh? Wha kens? I daenna.
But fine I ken the strauchtest thocht
can bend afore a ree and skinklan pun;
and no sae muckle flatterie o sel
to panse it skinkles—fowk aye state

90

"The pun 's the laichest form o wit," and wha
wad grudge me mastery o sic puir art?
No least masel—ma ain douce critic,
favourite and fere.
Ach, nae mair! Awa wi harnfash—
aa this cerebral Fanny Adams.
Aye, and no as gin I staun
sowldramman the glammert surrogate
o' Calton Hill—ma windflaucht, weet Parnassus.
Na, I staun here in Princes Street,
smirr faas, cars hiss by,
I'm dampt cauld and ma bus owre lang.
Myne, better this—than liggan deid
like Arnold—puir Empedocles Arnold
rinnan for a bus then crack—hertsnap
and his outraxan liquid gleid
cauldlava'd til a dwynan daud
far less substantial than the chad
on his ayebydan beach. . . .
"Come luve, let us be leal"—
Aye, there's a thocht, but gey, gey cauldrife
gin there was nae luve—just makars' anodyne,
and certies, thon's smaa comfort.
Luve? Whit's luve? A la Wedo, Wife o Bath,
Heloise, Elizabeth B., Brynhild, Madie Smith,
Clarinda? Whaur's the equation? Wha can fix . . . ?
Havers! Harnfash! Panse hou Burns,
that raucle calculator, aince
in this guid city jottit doun
the mathematics o his hert and loins
for nae mair lear than wha 'll equate
the whispert sang, the fleeran snigger—
and aa sae comical!
Ree, ramskeerie, tapsalteerie,
Clarinda birlan frae the dreich—
glinkan, douce and couthie lassie,
ae fond kiss and she'd hae screicht. . . .

91

To Hel wi Brynhild, Arnold, Burns—
that haill pack 's mair substantial than
ma feet fast dwynan
til a freezan daud. . . .
Dunedin—Edinburgh—Dunburgh.
A gey done burgh? Wha cares!
Here 's my bus.

gey—very; kens—knows; daenna—don't; strauchtest thocht—straightest thought; ree—high-spirited; skinklan—sparkling; panse—think; laichest—lowest; sic puir—such poor; douce—gentle; fere—friend; harnfash—mental conflict; aa—all; sowldramman—taking refreshment from a sympathetic environment; glammert—spellbound; windflaucht—gusty; smirr—drizzle; myne—mind; outraxan—outstretching; gleid—flame; cauldlava'd—cooled and thickened as lava does in becoming basalt; dwynan—wasting away; daud—lump; chad—small stones; ayebydan—eternal; leal—loyal; cauldrife—chilly; makars—poets; certies—certainly; havers—nonsense; raucle—fearless; aince—once; lear—learning; ramskeerie—wild, restless; tapsalteerie—topsy-turvy; birlan—spinning; dreich—dull; glinkan—jilting; couthie—well-to-do; screicht—screeched; haill—whole.

GILES GORDON b. 1940

A FORMER LOVE

She grew from the crowd,
stepping, streaming along the pavement,
head tossed high,
hair longer than before.
She saw me,
swooped head to breast,
rushed past.

A scent hung in the air.

WEST CORK

The landscape recedes, is illusory.
Mist falls, rises; hangs like an overcoat
or groundsheet, blocking out movement, sight lines.

On a hot day donkeys and a white horse
nibble and graze; cows chew; fowl scratch and cluck;
a heavy pig snorts, grunts, moves like a bomb.

Sea sparkles, islands stipple the water,
yellow broom sings out from vegetation,
bluebells, daisies, primroses, ferns, all smile.

Men and women like giants move through fields,
along lanes. This way they work, this way live.
Their being has good reason, better rhythm.

When the sun has sunk they go, disappear.
So do the animals. The land empties,
is hundreds of shades of green, and vacant.

Did you imagine them, those that you saw?
Their houses have melted into the hills,
the smoke from the chimneys merged with the mist.

The landscape remains. You hear a dog bark,
seagulls squawk, fresh water gush through a stream,
waves lick at the rocks. You feel the wind bite.

ELEGY

I. M. ORLANDO TOBIAS GORDON
born Charing Cross Hospital, 5 p.m., 8 August 1967
died Fulham Hospital, 8 p.m., 8 August 1967

1.

For moments she didn't recognise me:
white rubber boots, green coat, mouth and nose pad,
a linen cap. They had me hold her arm,
press a mask to her face to help her breathe.
They strapped her legs up high, covered the limbs
with green leggings, laid green all over her.
She resembled the contours and colours
of distant County Cork, without passion.

The baby when it came was wet and red,
was whisked away from my sight, more so hers,
before colour could be confirmed. (Thank God.)
It lay within its glass case on green cloth,
which also covered its parts. Its colour
was milk chocolate from lack of oxygen.
Green and brown, landscape, equator colours,
surprising pigments for a white baby.

2.

Were three hours in this world enough for you?
One hour for each month premature perhaps?
For months you'd swum inside your water sack,
throbbed and banged and made your existence felt.
If you'd stood the pace, waited for three months,
you'd have seen the world. It could wait for you.

94

There would have been thousands upon thousands
of babies born before you, now to then.
And thousands and thousands of people dead.

Were three hours enough? Is our world so dull
or horrible that you would rather sleep
for all time, having a name and three hours?
Oh how you hurt her, how you have hurt her!
For so long, for such a short time to stay.
I thought you were dead when they drew you out:
you were so silent, no noise, just the mess.
I saw you as you came, your gory head
first, and noticed only baby, not sex
or size. Two hours later I looked again,
having been to Lyons for egg and tea.
You lay in your glass case, breathing wildly
through tubes, and tubes, and tubes; or so it seemed.

And they covered your body and hid you
from me, or what *you* did not wish to see.
Our world is difficult, short of meaning.
If there is a God, then there is a God.
To me you are dead. I am so detached
from you now that I still see you breathing
in your tent, your perfect features so small,
yet a miniature version of a man.
Such perfection could not stand our air long.

3.

On the kitchen table, household objects
to do with living: a bread knife and board,
two green saucers, a packet of Corn Flakes,
a saucepan lid; coffee beans, sugar, rice,
lentils and salt in glass jars; cooking oil:
a blue and white striped jug filled with lemon

juice, mixed with water. Half the dead lemon
lies on the table, squeezed, dry and empty.
Also two packets of "The Iron Tablets,"
with instructions: "Take one tablet with meals,
three times a day throughout your pregnancy:
this is important to ensure that you
do not become anaemic." And a watch.

On the kitchen table, household objects
to do with dying. The watch has run down.
This still life has been untouched for three days.
There has been no living, only dying
in another place. The Iron Tablets are
an anachronism now, the lemon
and its juice squeezed unnecessarily.
There is no baby. There will not be one.
There was a baby. It breathed for three hours.
All there is to show is her flat stomach,
death and birth certificates, an empty
house. The watch stopped at when the breathing did.
The still life will be still for weeks longer.

W. S. GRAHAM b. 1917

From THE DARK DIALOGUES

II.

Almost I, yes, I hear
Huge in the small hours
A man's step on the stair
Climbing the pipeclayed flights
And then stop still
Under the stairhead gas

At the lonely tenement top.
The broken mantle roars
Or dims to a green murmur.
One door faces another.
Here, this is the door
With the loud grain and the name
Unreadable in brass.
Knock, but a small knock,
The children are asleep.
I sit here at the fire
And the children are there
And in this poem I am,
Their mother through his mother.
I sit with the gas turned
Down and time knocking
Somewhere through the wall.
Wheesht, children, and sleep
As I break the raker up,
It is only the stranger
Hissing in the grate.
Only to speak and say
Something, little enough,
Not out of want,
Nor out of love, to say
Something and to hear
That someone has heard me.
This is the house I married
Into, a room and kitchen
In a grey tenement,
The top flat of the land,
And I hear them breathe and turn
Over in their sleep
As I sit here becoming
Hardly who I know.
I have seen them hide
And seek and cry come out
Come out whoever you are

You're not het I called
And called across the wide
Wapenshaw of water.
But the place moved away
Beyond the reach of any
Word. Only the dark
Dialogues drew their breath.
Ah how bright the mantel
Brass shines over me.
Black-lead at my elbow,
Pipe-clay at my feet.
Wheesht and go to sleep
And grow up but not
To say mother mother
Where are the great games
I grew up quick to play.

III.

Now in the third voice
I am their father through
Nothing more than where
I am made by this word
And this word to occur.
Here I am makeshift made
By artifice to fall
Upon a makeshift time.
But I can't see. I can't
See in the bad light
Moving (is it moving?)
Between your eyes and mine.
Who are you and yet
To find the side of the road,
My head inclined, my ears
Feathered to every wind
Blown between the dykes.

The mist is coming home.
I hear the blind horn
Mourning from the firth.
The big wind blows
Over the shore of my child-
Hood in the off season.
The small wind remurmurs
The fathering tenement
And a boy I knew running
The hide and seeking streets.
Or do these winds
In their forces blow
Between the words only?

I am the shell held
To Time's ear and you
May hear the lonely leagues
Of the kittiwake and the fulmar.

IV.

Or am I always only
Thinking is this the time
To look elsewhere to turn
Towards what was it
I put myself out
Away from home to meet?
Was it this only? Surely
It is more than these words
See on my side
I went halfway to meet.

And there are other times.
But the times are always
Other and now what I meant
To say or hear or be

Lies hidden where exile
Too easily beckons.
What if the terrible times
Moving away find
Me in the end only
Staying where I am always
Unheard by a fault.

So to begin to return
At last neither early
Nor late and go my way
Somehow home across
This gesture become
Inhabited out of hand.
I stop and listen over
My shoulder and listen back
On language for that step
That seems to fall after
My own step in the dark.

Always must be the lost
Or where we turn, and all
For a sight of the dark again.
The farthest away, the least
To answer back come nearest.

And this place is taking
Its time from us though these
Two people or voices
Are not us nor has
The time they seem to move in
To do with what we think
Our own times are. Even
Where we are is only
This one inhuman place.
Yet somewhere a stone
Speaks and maybe a leaf

In the dark turns over.
And whoever I meant
To think I had met
Turns away further
Before me blinded by
This word and this word.

See how presently
The bull and the girl turn
From what they seemed to say
And turn there above me
With that star-plotted head
Snorting on silence.
The legend turns. And on
Her starry face descried
Faintly astonishment.
The formal meadow fades
Over the ever-widening
Firth and in their time
That not unnatural pair
Turn slowly home.

This is no other place
Than where I am, between
This word and the next.
Maybe I should expect
To find myself only
Saying that again
Here now at the end.
Yet over the great
Gantries and cantilevers
Of love, a sky, real and
Particular, is slowly
Startled into light.

YOUNG POLITICIAN

What a lovely, lovely moon.
And it's in the constituency too.

THE NEWTON MAN

an irritable man   a grumpy humphie
squared by reason   ringed by fact
shock-proof   disaster-ridden
crank-turning   inch devouring
tickle tensing   tally hoing
vital no   statistics yes

who organises the discovery of matter?
microscopic caligulas devilish exmechanics
accumulators and cross reference men
lonely plagiarisers in guggenheim monasteries
icecold schizoids in the dungeons of gridgraph

lady godiva had moles on her molecules
and peeping tom won the nobel prize for minute
      observation

THE WORSTEST BEAST

the worstest beast that swims in the sea
is man with his bathing trunks down to his knee

the worstest beast that goes through the air
is man with his comb to tidy his hair

the worstest beast that bores through soil
is man with his uses for metal and oil

the worstest beast that hunts for meat
is man who kills and does not eat

the worstest beast that suckles its young
is man who's scared of nipples and dung

the worstest beast that copulates
is man who's mixed his loves and hates

the worstest beast that has warm skin
is man who stones himself with sin

he's the worstest beast because he's won
it's a master race and it's almost run

PERSON

i have no thumb
i am a little
deformed

i don't wear gloves
but i suffer very much
from the insolence
of those who are thumbed
and find in that
their distinction

MOON

they were arguing over the dead lady's body
the surgeon said
    freeze her. give me ten years
    and unlimited money
    for certain machines
    she will walk, breathe
the man from the funeral parlour said
    that is obscene
    with my hands i will give her beauty and peace
    more than is fair
    she will stay loved in the dreams
    of us trapped in air
when i hurried into the bed and said
    bells confetti priest cake
    i'm marrying future and past now
    and this is the one i take

NOTICE

in the outposts of the dark
the long weeds the tattered frags
in the tumble down stand still wreck
of tolerance and easy going
I
am muted
a ring lost from a dead queen
    I am parted from the other
because I'm playing
been very human

for too long
dandled everybody
it's not been my way to be bitter and savage in a pub
but from now on
I AM NOT IN

what a hateful arrogant man
not to be in

but that's the notice I'm giving.

WAS A SHAME

Was a shame for my mum that to make me well
I had to give her bloody hell.

She'd had the blood of my birth before
Couldn't she suffer this one more?

Far from wanting my second birth
She tried to hold me fast to the earth.

It's a pity she hadn't the heart to be glad
Her kid had guts as good as his dad.

But she hadn't and, friend, I'm no Christian fool.
I firmly believe you've got to be cruel to be cruel.

By Christ I kicked her where it hurt her most.
The noise of her screams is still my boast.

I jumped on her belly until her bones rang,
And as I jumped I danced and sang.

And the song I sang was of a fire
That flamed up into a bird of desire.

And the bird of desire flew in the sky
Until it turned to heaven's eye.

And heaven's eye shone in the night
And filled the earth with a birthday light.

And that birthday light was a sign for me
To leap off my mum and be free, be free.

And now, born again, no longer sick,
I kiss my mother and never kick.

THREE LITTLE GREEN QUARTERS

There's leafs and pools inside to hide in
skins and pods and shells to slide in
there's barks and musk and sands to touch
lots of things in us not human very much
if we want
but we don't but only a few do
for the rest the past is mumbo hoodoo
something sucked and scaled
been transcended
a gold rush trail that's been hauled and ended

i and myself would like to sink into the non
human to the eyes

pleasure of vision the only prize
but know very well the other guys
wont give up their lust
to organize
          dissect dead flies
and get ten men working on another man's whys
they're all at it and out
                up and on
eager to get the whole universe mapped
not sensing the pulse of their guts is gone
just as if the spinal cord had snapped
they've not felt yet they're spinning in space
running in no race
just black
sheep shot out from home in disgrace
to make good or get lost in a distant place
to be forgotten in any case
but the signs that our minds roam on untied lines
are there in what we're wishing for
a martian year one
in our nineteen eighty four
a meeting with strange captains from a master civilization
who will bend gently over us through galactic curves
and offer what they've learned in an older universe
to help us through our long division
the conquerors of matter
and the absurds of evolution

meanwhile we discover in earth's skies at night
the unidentified flying object guilt
the beautiful round shining space ship god
the dark fast dangerous cigar shape the devil
and the appearance and eclipse in a flash of red
of three little green quarters of our personality
near an ancient burial ground just inside our head.

WILLIE'S SHETLAND-BOAT

It were as if the mould
was the trough of a wave
taken by the eye to the land
and by the hand filled around
with larch. First with adze
he carved out the wooden keel
to lie as heavy flotsam
against the drag of the sea,
and then with the template bowed
the strakes like swans' wings
from stem to stern, and finally
he cut the ribs—a wishbone
for their flight.

From the same wave she was made
as the Gokstad ship, but Willie's hand
and Willie's eye saw only
the haaf grounds and the mind
to reach them and return
with the speed of the fulmar
before that wave
reclaimed its stolen shape.

FISHERMAN

He sails at night
or in cold dawns, whether
the sky be red or the fat moon

palls at its reflection. His hands
are mullets, hanging head-down
from his sleeves and his face
you would judge slapped
once too often
by the sea's salt canvas.

He swims in oilskins on the deck,
a wet uncle to the scales
threshing blue and silver
maelstroms from the nets.
He does not sing shanties nor
jigs about the ropes—but swearing
curses the freezing lumps of water
—or silent lies deader
in his bunk than any fish.

BLIND MAN IN A BASEMENT

Through the curtains
of a basement window
a blind man learned to see,

By sound and rhythm of pace,
by inflection and accent of step
—who passed.

A high-heeled click. Is she
young and beautiful?
—listen!

The hesitancy, the lightness
—she must be.

Compare it with the loping
stride of crêpe and leather.
Somebody tall with ease
or short,
stretching himself downhill.

The speed with which they leave
my ears, he said,
is my yardstick for age;
and the speed
with which they leave my thoughts
my touchstone for beauty.

And the ones I cannot guess at
—don't know themselves.

JOHN KINCAID b. 1909

THE BACKEND OF POLITICS

Cauld and dour as a Janiver wind
the efter-braith o het rebellion,
when aa the wheel o airn aiths
turns birlygaun o shibboleths. . . .

Wyce chiel, thocht I,
and followed the staur
owre ben and muir
til airts gey faur.
But when I cam
til the Inn itsel
nae jizzen huid been,
nae dounset hell,

nae folk aa roun
a fey wean's crib,
kennin their days
til heaven's were sib.
Ilk room wuis fou
o commissar chiels,
clashin o luve
and fetchin like deils.
I lookit up. . . .
'twuis as I feared,
the staur itsel
huid disappeared.

Cauld and dour as a Janiver wind
the eftercome o the hert's rebellion,
when aa the speik o the reid reithe mou
turns clishmaclaver o shibboleths.

cauld—cold; *dour*—severe; *Janiver*—January; *efter-braith*—after-breath;
het—hot; *aa*—all; *airn aiths*—iron oaths; *birlygaun*—spinning round;
wyce—knowing; *chiel*—fellow; *thocht*—thought; *airts*—directions; *jizzen*
—child-bed; *dounset*—overpowered; *fey*—doomed; *wean*—child; *sib*—
akin; *fou*—full; *clashin*—tattling; *fechtin*—fighting; *deils*—devils; *'twuis*—
'twas; *eftercome*—sequel; *speik*—speech; *reid reithe mou*—red ardent
mouth; *clishmaclaver*—idle talk.

A MAKAR'S TALE

On a Setterday's morn
I lowped the wame
and took the breist
and got a name.

Through Sunday's daurkness I keeked out,
bumbaized, on the gaitherin daw,

and heard aa fairheid pipe its flute
owre the chimbleys and awa.
Eh, sicna gowd wuis near my haun,
but near my feckless haun in vain;
I gazed, but couldna understaun,
maist like a puddock on a stane.

On Monday the mongers dinged me doun
and gien me bitter breid;
and while I tholed the dirlin stoun
they girned attour my heid.
Sae I pentit the staurs wi anger's reid,
and cled my hert wi thorns o whin,
and merrit my lass in a daftsome tid,
and coost my caidie owre the mune.

On Tuesday aabody gaed til war,
and if them, why no me?
Sae they flung me til ane eastlin staur,
and damn my poesie!
But the staur bleezed up wi fremit fire,
the desert daunsed wi micht and main,
and, brekin the heart wi wud desire,
yonner wuis fairheid's flute again.

Owre Wednesday's lyft sic phantoms flew
my haun wuis graithed to scrieve,
but a fit o freens caa'd out "Halloo!"
and virr frae me did rieve.
I took the dominie's road til schule,
I buried my dool in ten times ten,
but ilk time makar maks his will
fairheid's flute 's in the mou o a wean . . .

Thursday's here, and I maun wake,
fling the cerements o nicht
out o my heid for scrievin's sake,

seek aye and aye for licht.
For licht maun come (though freens may gae)
and catch the makar's lane nainsel
on 's Claudius knees, wi Hamlet's wae
pyntin the richt reithe road til hell.

> On whitna day
> will deid claim me?
> Pray life itsel
> willna main me!

T. S. LAW b. 1910

IMPORTANCE

He daesnae juist drap a name
or set it up and say grace wi 't,
he lays it oot on his haun
and hits ye richt in the face wi 't.

Generous tho, tae a faut.
Ay, no a ticht man, no mean wi 't.
Gie him anither chance
and he'll hit ye atween the een wi 't.

THE HERO

Gin Cuchulain had never been, nor thon lustre o his days,
the heroics o his devoirs bleezin fae his broo lik the rays
o the ayebydein staur caad Ireland, there 'd never hae been
the sang tae sing it, nor the singer tae inspire
the lieges even-on thru years as green
wi hope as the machair wi the rain, or as ruid wi the fire
o anger as the sea wi the wastren sun can show it:
it's a paer bit growthe that has nae grund alow it.

Lea them alane, the folk, juist let them byde
lik the gress for the feck o three thoosan year an mair,
whyles growein like a steerin laddie, whyles ill-guidit,
a lad o pairts but the pairts gey ill-dividit,
but aye abuin aathing, thursel, that nocht can hyde,
no even the desolatioun o despair.

devoirs bleezin—duties blazing; *ayebydein staur*—everlasting star; *caad*—
called; *machair*—shore; *ruid*—red; *paer*—poor; *alow*—below; *lea*—leave;
whyles—sometimes; *steerin laddie*—lively boy; *abuin aathing*—above
everything; *thursel*—themselves; *nocht*—nothing.

MAURICE LINDSAY b. 1918

STONES IN SKY AND WATER

Under the lap of water sunken stones change
their indefinable shapes. A dazzle gleams
from the roof-tops of ripples. Summer's bright-
ness peoples the loch with moveless stir that seems
to mingle height and distance. Clouds free-range,

trailing their aimless shadows. Water's peace
gets rubbed against by winds that peel off light.
But the smooth-bending forms the stones release
float upwards like cast images, to exchange
the appearance for reality and spring
fresh impulses, the flux of all delight
a moment in eternity can bring
when stones in sky and water silently sing.

EARLY MORNING FISHER

Stubbed at the pond's edge, blunted by his pipe,
his eyes are lined to the rod he strings and flails
through delicate arcs that flick the air with water.
Posing its own question, a swan sails
over its answers. Unconcerned, its mate
glides from the rushes, visibling the breeze
that shifts the thin mist blenched from the back of
    darkness
to kindle dawn among the smoking trees.

Day broadens. The fisherman spreads his patience
angled only to tense and trap the bite
slashing the pond's translucence, sliver-knife
that flashes cold through cunning out of sight,
the pulse in that green-bottled ooze of life
each morning lairs afresh with a rocking light.

AT HANS CHRISTIAN ANDERSEN'S BIRTHPLACE, ODENSE, DENMARK

Sunlight folds back pages of quiet shadows
against the whitewashed walls of his birthplace.
                                        Tourists move
through crowded antiseptic rooms and ponder
what row after row of glass-cased papers ought to prove.

Somehow the long-nosed gangling boy who was only
at home in fairy-land, has left no clues.
The tinder-box of Time we rub
answers us each the way we choose.

For kings have now no daughters left for prizes.
Swineherds remain swineherds; not a spell
can make the good man prince; psychiatrists
have dredged up wonder from the wishing well.

The whole of his terrible, tiny world might be
dismissed as a beautiful madman's dream, but that each
    of us knows
whenever we move out from the warmth of our loneliness
we may be wearing the Emperor's new clothes.

THIS BUSINESS OF LIVING

Midges fasten their mist-cloud over the river,
zizzing and zazzing, stitching intricacy,
an uncolliding shimmer, a pattern
that satisfies some midge necessity.

A wind, shuttling through roots of weeds and grasses,

side-slips against the weave of their symmetry
and breaks its shape. The rupture shifts, is mended,
then suddenly struck by a thrust of energy

the water twists up out of its element;
a kick of trout that heels midges from air,
recoiling under its own ripples, leaving
torn suspension, a gapped bite to repair.

Immediately the chromosomes reshuffle
to push the mist-cloud back to its old form
and I, on the bank, experience satisfaction
watching a small completeness assert its norm.

AT THE MOUTH OF THE ARDYNE

The water rubs against itself,
glancing many faces at me.
One winces as the dropped fly
tears its tension. Then it heals.

Being torn doesn't matter.
The water just goes on saying
all that water has to say,
what the dead come back to.

Then a scar opens.
Something of water is ripped out,
a struggle with swung air.
I batter it on a loaf of stone.

The water turns passing faces,
innumerable pieces of silver.
I wash my hands, pack up, and

go home wishing I hadn't come.

Later, I eat my guilt.

SMALL BOY WRITING

My little son beside me shapes his letters,
a tremulous M, a not-quite-meeting O,
sticking them with his breath down careful pages,
    row on repeated row.

He'll heir the questions elder, self-styled betters
have jumbled from these same laborious signs,
and find what somehow answered for their ages
    has slipped between the lines:

their lingered creeds and dogmas, slackened fetters
no longer strong enough to hold the mind
back from its baffled necessary sieges,
    though nothing 's there behind.

He'll find how little we are still their debtors,
their purposes unpurposed, doubts secured
without assurances, their faith's self-pledges,
    lonelinesses endured.

So may he learn resistance to go-getters
prospecting ends and absolutes; be content
to take delight's quick shapes and sudden edges
    as living's monument.

PICKING APPLES

Apple time, and the trees brittle with fruit.
My children climb the bent, half-sapping branches
to where the apples, cheeked with the hectic flush
of Autumn, hang. The children bark their haunches

and lean on the edge of their balance. The apples are out
of reach; so they shake the tree. Through a tussle of leaves
    and laughter
the apples thud down; thud on the orchard grasses
in rounded, grave finality, each one after

the other dropping; the muffled sound of them dropping
like suddenly hearing the beats of one's own heart
falling away, as if shaken by some storm
as localised as this. Loading them into the cart,

the sweet smell of their bruises moist in the sun,
their skins' bloom tacky against the touch,
I experience fulfilment, suddenly aware
of some ripe, wordless answer, knowing no such

answers exist; only questions, questions, the beating years,
the dropped apples . . the kind of touch and go
that poetry makes satisfactions of;
reality, with nothing more to show

than a brush of branches, time and the apples falling,
and shrill among the leaves, my children impatiently
    calling.

GLASGOW NOCTURNE

Materialised from the flaked stones of buildings
dank with neglect and poverty, the pack,
thick-shouldered, slunk through rows of offices
squirting anonymous walls with their own lack

of self-identity. *Tong ya bass, Fleet,*
Fuck the Pope spurted like blood: a smear
protesting to the passing daylight folk
the prowled-up edge of menace, the spoor of fear

that many waters cannot quench, or wash
clean from what hands, what eyes, from what hurt hearts?
O Lord! the preacher posed at the park gates,
what must we do to be whole in all our parts?

Late on Saturday night, when shopfronts doused
their furniture, contraceptives, clothes and shoes,
violence sneaked out in banded courage,
bored with hopelessness that has nothing to lose.

A side-street shadow eyed two lovers together;
he, lured from the loyalties of the gang
by a waif who wore her sex like a cheap trinket;
she, touched to her woman's need by his wrong

tenderness. On the way from their first dance,
the taste of not enough fumbled their search
of hands and lips endeared in a derelict close.
Over the flarepath of their love, a lurch

thrust from the shadow, circling their twined bodies.
It left them clung before its narrowing threat
till she shrieked. They peeled her from her lover,
a crumpled sob of a doll dropped in the street,

while he received his lesson: ribs and jaw
broken, kidneys and testicles ruptured, a slit
where the knife licked his groin. Before he died
in the ambulance, she'd vanished. Shops lit

up their furniture, contraceptives, clothes and shoes
again. Next morning, there was a darker stain
than *Tong ya bass* and *Fleet* on the edge of the kerb;
but it disappeared in the afternoon rain.

A BALLAD OF ORPHEUS

On the third day after her unexpected death,
Orpheus descended into Hell.
It wasn't hard to find. He knew the directions well,
asleep, he'd often read them by the light of his own breath.

The doorkeeper was surly, but let him in;
he had no reason to keep anyone out.
Glaring like a lit city, a kind of visible shout
fungused about the place, an absolute din

of all notes, overtones and unheard sounds at once.
To keep his sense of self intact, he struck
a few familiar chords, and as his luck
would have it, she, who all along had felt a hunch

something unusual would happen, heard the order
and limiting purpose of his playing; and being not yet
fully subtracted out of herself to fit
Hell's edgeless ambiguities, broke from the border

of blurring dissolution, and moved towards her lover
as a cloud might move in the world of gods above.
He guessed that shape and stir to be his love
Eurydice, well knowing that no other

idea of woman would answer to the lyre
that sang against his loins. She came to him crying
aloud her numbed womanly tenderness, trying
to warm her cold half-body at the core of his fire.

But without a word said, he seized her hand
and began pulling her roughly along the road,
past the doorkeeper, who smirked, seeing the load
he carried. She, being a woman, couldn't understand

that love in action needs no drag of speech,
and pled with him to turn round once and kiss
her. Of all the conditions the gods had imposed, this
was the one he dared not disobey. Reproach

followed reproach; till, as he fled
through shadow to shadow, suddenly it seemed
that the only absolute good was what he'd dreamed
of her. So Orpheus stopped, and slowly turned his head.

At once she began to small. He watched her disappear
backwards away from him, and thought it best
that things should be so. How could he have stood the test
of constant loving, always with the fear

of his first loss ahead of him again,
believing happiness ends in boredom or pain?
So Orpheus returned by the same lane
as he went down by, to compose himself in a world of men.

But there 's a sequel to this traveller's tale.
The Thracian women, sensing the need to purge
his unfulfilment of the sexual urge,
tore his manhood apart, and with a wail

that made even Hell's distant doorkeeper tremble,
threw his warm parts onto the legendary floods.
The warning here to all you whole young bloods
who go out after women is: don't dissemble.

CRIONADH

Dh'fhiosraich thu an toiseach
tòisich
rathad a dh'fhosgail
air gach taobh;
blàthan, ann a' mios na gréine,
a driaman do cheum
is 'na do shùil.

Cheannsaich thu mhaise
annad le stuaimeachd;
mhùch thu faicsinn
is a riadh;
choisich thu an dubhar cràbhaidh;
thog thu gàrradh
mu do ghrian.

Latha, deireadh foghar
bruidhteach,
thugadh ceum leat,
le cinn chrom;
rinneadh an t-slighe leat gu dìreach;
's cha dug thu sùil
a-nall no null.

WITHERING

You experienced at the very start a way that opened on all
sides, blossoms in the sun's regard in the maze of your steps
and in your eyes.

You mastered that beauty with moderation, you stifled vision and its reward, you walked in a religious shade, around your sun you built a wall.

One day after a bruising autumn they walked you out, their heads bowed low, they took you by the straightest route, and you looked not after or before.

COMHARRA STIUIRIDH

Siud an t-eilean ás an t-sealladh
mar a shiùbhlas am bàta
mar a chunnaic iomadh bàrd e
eadar liunn is iargan,
's fir eil' a bha 'n teanga fo fiacaill,
's deòir a' dalladh
dùbhradh neo-dhearbht is uinneagan a' fannadh

Ach chan eil a' cheiste cho sìmplidh
do 'n allmharach an comhair na bliadhna
a-mach á tilleadh éiridh iargan
á roinn a chuir an saoghal an dìmeas.

Cuideachd, chan e siud m' eilean-s';
chaidh esan fodha o chionn fhada,
a' chuid mhór dheth,
fo dheireas is ainneart;
's na chaidh fodha annam fhìn dheth,
'na ghrianan 's cnoc eighre
tha e a' seòladh na mara anns am bì mi
'na phrìomh chomharr stiùiridh
cunnartach, do-sheachaint, gun fhaochadh.

LANDMARK

There goes the island out of sight as the boat sails on, as seen by many a bard through sorrow and beer and by others, tongue under tooth, and tears blinding—an ill-defined shadow and windows fading.

But the matter is not so simple to the one who's a yearly pilgrim out of returning sorrow rises from a region the world has derided.

And, that is not my island; it submerged long ago, the greater part of it, in neglect and tyranny—and the part that submerged in me of it, sun-bower and iceberg, sails the ocean I am in a primary landmark, dangerous, essential, demanding.

ATH-ARMACHADH. . . . AN REUSANACHADH

"Sgrios"
ars esan,
"'s eadh, mur eil an còrr air a shon,
gus an Rìoghachd thoirt gu buil,
ach sprèadhadh is sgrios
is fuil."

"Is có" ars esan
"e—
am fear tha gus innse
an staid air am bì An Rìoghachd
'na ainm ach
A fear fhéin: am
Fìrean;

"is có" ars esan,
"e—
am fear a tha gus innse

có am fear air am bì Am Fìrean
'na ainm ach
(có eile?) Am
Fìrean."

Is bheir Am Fìrean
arm dhan an Fhìrean
air chùmhnant An Rìoghachd thoirt gu buil
—gun mhios
air cosg eadar luime
is sgrios
gu ruig an cruinne–
cé. . . .
Gun teagamh
cuiridh sin casg air
a 'Pheacadh'—
cha bhì rìoghachd ann

("ach An Rìoghachd. . . . .")

RE-ARMAMENT. . . . THE REASONING

"Destruction" he said "Yes, if there is no other way, for the Kingdom to be fulfilled but disintegration, destruction, and blood."

"And who," said he, "is the one who is to say what state will have The Kingdom for a name but its own man; The Righteous;"

"And who" said he "is the one who is to say what man will have The Righteous for a name but (who else?) The Righteous."

And The Righteous will issue arms to The Righteous commanding that The Kingdom be fulfilled—regardless of cost in desolation and destruction sparing not even the world . . . Truly that will master "Sin"—there will be no kingdom left

("But the Kingdom. . . .")

Dh'fhuiling thu fanaid
agus tàmailt,
bha thu 'na do chùis-bhùirt is magaidh—
nan canadh tu facal
bhathas dha mar
shùlaire gu comharr mara.

Bha thu 'na do chulaidh ìobairt
air na rinn do luchd-baile
(saoilidh
mi) an luchd peacaidh fhàgail;
's bu shuarach aca–
san an lochd
a chuireadh 'na do thosd thu leth ràidhe.

Ach theasbain thu rud eile dhòmhsa—
bha m' eòlas-s' ort eadar-dhealaicht
dh'fhiosraich mi taobh chaoin do nàduir:
b' e sin bàigh is
teang' ealant;
bha thu buailte ann an càradh

as na dh'fhoghlaim mi gum pàidhear
caoine agus ealantas
le tàire—
's cha bu mhisde mi an earail
nach eil duais is duine coimhliont.

. . . . . A-bhòin-dé fhuair thu bàs;
leig iad a-mach thu air an uinneig;
ceannruisgte
thog iad thu an àirde—
modh is àit agad mu dheireadh.

DELICATE BALANCE

You suffered ignominy and shame; target for slight and mock-
ery—each word you spoke they dived upon like gannets sighting
fish.

Your rôle was sacrificial, a symbol for your fellows (it seems
to me) to cast their sins upon, and they cared nothing for the
harm that, half a season, left you dumb.

But you meant something else to me, I had different knowledge
of you, the person I experienced was warm with elegant tongue :
you were limited by a plight from which I learned that men
repay art and tenderness with spite and I lost nothing from the
precept that a man and his fate are disparate. . . .

The day before yesterday you died; they let you out through
the window; bare-headed they raised you on high—you had a
place and respect in the end.

GEORGE MACBETH b. 1932

THE WASP'S NEST

All day to the loose tile behind the parapet
The droning bombers fled : in the wet gutter
Belly-upwards the dead were lying, numbed
By October cold. And now the bloat queen,
Sick-orange, with wings draped, and feelers trailing,
Like Helen combing her hair, posed on the ledge
Twenty feet above the traffic. I watched, just a foot
From her eyes, very glad of the hard glass parting
My pressed human nose from her angry sting
And her heavy power to warm the cold future

Sunk in unfertilised eggs. And I thought: if I reached
And inched this window open, and cut her in half
With my unclasped pen-knife, I could exterminate
An unborn generation. All next summer,
If she survives, the stepped roof will swarm
With a jam of striped fighters. Therefore, this winter
In burning sulphur in their dug-out hangars
All the bred wasps must die. Unless I kill her.
So I balanced assassination with genocide
As the queen walked on the ledge, a foot from my eyes
In the last sun of the year, the responsible man
With a cold nose, who knew that he must kill,
Coming to no sure conclusion, nor anxious to come.

THE WARD

Along that ward men died each winter night.
        One in an iron lung
Used to cry out before that salving tin
Strapped round his breathing stifled him. One hung
        In a strange brace
That moved his dead leg gently. And no light
        Out of that blaze where Hitler in
His burning concrete died lit the cramped face

Of a boy paralysed. I in that war
        Lay with cold steel on wrists
Recording how my heart beat, saved and one
With the men dying. Dark amidst the mists
        Across the seas
Each night in France those armies gripped and tore

  Each other's guts out, and no sun
Arched in at dawn through stiff windows to tease

Men left in pain. Sisters on morning rounds
　　　Brought laundered sheets and screens
Where they were needed. And when doctors came
In clean coats with their talk and their machines,
　　　Behind their eyes
Moving to help, what was there? To the sounds
　　　Of distant gunfire, in our name,
So many men walked into death. What lies

And festers is the wastage. Here the beast
　　　Still breathes its burning stone
And claws the entrails. And those hours of cold
When I lay waking, hearing men alone
　　　Fight into death
Swim back and grip. And I feel rise like yeast
　　　A sense of the whole world grown old
With no one winning. And I fight for breath.

THE SHELL

Since the shell came and took you in its arms
　　　Whose body was fine bone
That walked in light beside a place of flowers,
　　　Why should your son
Years after the eclipse of those alarms
　　　Perplex this bitten stone
For some spent issue of the sea? Not one
Blue drop of drying blood I could call ours

In all that ocean that you were remains
　　　To move again. I come
Through darkness from a distance to your tomb
　　　And feel the swell

Where a dark flood goes headlong to the drains.
I hear black hailstones drum
Like cold slugs on your skin. There is no bell
To tell what drowned king founders. Violets bloom

Where someone died. I dream that overhead
    I hear a bomber drone
And feel again stiff pumping of slow guns
    Then the All Clear's
Voice break, and the long summing of the dead
    Below the siren's moan
Subdue the salt flood of all blood and tears
To a prolonged strained weeping sound that stuns.

I turn in anger. By whatever stars
    Clear out of drifting rack
This winter evening I revive my claim
    To what has gone
Beyond your dying fall. Through these cold bars
    I feel your breaking back
And live again your body falling on
That flood of stone where no white Saviour came

On Christian feet to lift you to the verge
    Or swans with wings of fire
Whose necks were arched in mourning. Black as coal
    I turn to go
Out of the graveyard. Headstone shadows merge
    And blur. I see the spire
Lift over corpses, and I sense the flow
Of death like honey to make all things whole.

THE RETURN

After the light has set

First I imagine silence: then the stroke
As if some drum beat outside has come in.
And in the silence I smell moving smoke
And feel the touch of coarse cloth on my skin.
 And all is darkness yet
Save where the hot wax withers by my chin.

 When I had fallen (bone
Bloodying wet stone) he would lead me back
Along the street and up the corkscrew stair
(Time running anti-clockwise, fingers slack)
And open windows to let in fresh air
 And leave me stretched alone
With sunken cheeks drained whiter than my hair.

 Then I was young. Before
Another stroke he will come back in bone
And thin my heart. That soot-black hill will break
And raise him in his clay suit from the stone
While my chalk-ridden fingers dryly ache
 And burn. On this rush floor
He will come striding hotly. When I wake

 The stroke will have been tolled
And I shall take his crushed purse in my hand
And feel it pulse (warm, empty) on my wrist.
Blood floods my temples. Clay man, from what land
 With someone grown so old?
Soldier, forgive me. Candles die in mist.

 And now a cold wind stirs
Inside the shuttered room. I feel his hand
Brushing the stale air, feeling for my place
Across the phlegm-soaked pillows. I am sand
Threading a glass with slow and even pace
 And dying in my furs.
My father turns, with tears on his young face.

PYRENEAN MOUNTAIN HOUND

As if
absorbing the whole
heat of snow

into his noble
coat, he
lifts,

heavy-lidded, the
sombre
gaze

of a glacier—
liver,
knowing

not only how
to revive
the frozen

with brandy, but
what
being wanted means

ALSATIAN

And yet
without exactly the
appearance of

being violent,

that heavy
tail, tucked

under the firm
hind-quarters,
occasions

doubts about the
advisability
of treating

this law-dog
as if
he was really only

a sheep
in wolf's-
clothing.

A MYTH OF ORIGIN

When the man awoke in the morning air in the garden
    and stretched his arms, above his head there were petals
        of roses and blue-bells. And whether he stared at the flowers
            for a second or two in hatred and wonder, or closed

his eyes in a fit of puzzled anger, or fear,
    we shall never know: but the steady flow of worms
        like a pouring of serpents over his hairy toes
            and the reach and tickle of huge roots through his thighs

on the drying soil, we can surely imagine. And how
    the glossy pebble he lolled his head on stirred
        and went flying rapidly off, and the rough warm earth
            rubbed over his green fur shoulders, I think

we can safely infer. So we find the man on his feet
　　having blundered some distance with cut face and thorn-
　　　　prickled hands
　　　　to the rim of a pond, where he lies on his belly to look
　　　　　　if there's water inside. And the granite flags of the pond

as he leans to drink are abrading the cage of his ribs.
　　And the curling wire in the green cave of his crutch
　　　　is raw and enflamed. The world is a dangerous place
　　　　　　for someone scratched by the pliant spears of Iris

whenever he goes for a stroll. Is he happy hearing
　　the crashing female swish of their flags interweaving
　　　　all round him, or watching the shielded elaborate loving
　　　　　　of ladybirds on the open bed of a lime-leaf

by the side of a lily? Amid such divisions of leaves,
　　and pouting of buds, and the aching infusions of scent
　　　　from that bawdy house of blossom, at least the bees
　　　　　　are alive to the needs of the towering lupins and fox-
　　　　　　　　gloves,

but who is to his? There is no one for him to love.
　　So the man goes down on his knees each night in the soil
　　　　beneath the gross blooms of a dying peony
　　　　　　or a dripping lilac that bleeds on his naked head

and examines the lines on his palm, and the marks on the leaves,
　　and tries to think. And each evening the tears break
　　　　from his eyes, and the sun sets in a pool of gold,
　　　　　　and the ground is wet with a new rush of seed

in the spinning round of the world. The shape of a wound,
　　or the hole in a tree, or the white wings of the stork
　　　　and the god in the cradle mean nothing. Mankind is alone
　　　　　　in the dark garden, with only himself to love.

IN A SHRUBBERY

Acid responses are no answer to
A thunder thump or tickling drop of dew:
Nor any other kind—I see that, too.

Yet what we say of what we say we feel
Feels like the feeling, afterwards. We conceal
What's finished with, in words, and think it real.

Crammed to coincidence, the two things say
What makes a birthday and a dying day
A dewclap or a thunderdrop away.

SO MANY SUMMERS

Beside one loch, a hind's neat skeleton,
Beside another, a boat pulled high and dry:
Two neat geometries drawn in the weather:
Two things already dead and still to die.

I passed them every summer, rod in hand,
Skirting the bright blue or the spitting gray,
And, every summer, saw how the bleached timbers
Gaped wider and the neat ribs fell away.

Time adds one malice to another one—
Now you'd look very close before you knew
If it's the boat that ran, the hind went sailing.
So many summers, and I have lived them too.

A MAN IN MY POSITION

Hear my words carefully.
Some are spoken
not by me, but
by a man in my position.

What right has he
to use my mouth? I hate him
when he touches you
the wrong way.

Yet he loves you also,
this appalling stranger
who makes windows of my eyes.
You see him looking out.

Until he dies
of my love for you
hear my words carefully—
for who is talking now?

OLD EDINBURGH

Down the Canongate
down the Cowgate
go vermilion dreams
snake's tongues of bannerets
trumpets with words from their mouths
saying Praise me, praise me.

Up the Cowgate
up the Canongate
lice on the march
tar on the amputated stump
Hell speaking with the tongue of Heaven
a woman tied to the tail of a cart.

And history stands by a dark entry
with words from his mouth
that say Pity me, pity me
but never forgive.

FLOODED MIND

When the water fell
the trees rose up again
and fish stopped being birds
among the branches.

The trees were never the same again, though,
and the birds
often regarded him
with a very fishy eye
as he walked the policies of himself,
his own keeper.

Also, he was afraid to go fishing
in case he landed a fish
with feathers that would sing
in his net.

No wonder his eyes were
noticeboards saying
Private. Keep out.

THE RED WELL, HARRIS

The Red Well has gone.
Thirty years ago I filled pails from it
with a flashing dipper and floated
a frond of bracken in each
so that no splash of water should escape
from its jolting prison.

Where that eye of water once
blinked from the ground
now stands a gray house
filled with voices.

The house is solid. But
nothing will keep the children
in its happy prison
from scattering abroad, till
the house at last stands empty—
one drained well
on top of another.

ONE OF THE MANY DAYS

I never saw more frogs
than once at the back of Ben Dòrain.
Joseph-coated, they ambled and jumped
in the sweet marsh grass
like coloured ideas.

The river ran glass in the sun.
I waded in the jocular water
of Loch Lyon. A parcel of hinds

gave the V-sign with their ears, then
ran off and off till they were
cantering crumbs. I watched
a whole long day
release its miracles.

But clearest of all I remember
the Joseph-coated frogs
amiably ambling or
jumping into the air—like
coloured ideas
tinily considering
the huge concept of Ben Dòrain.

SOUNDS OF THE DAY

When a clatter came,
It was horses crossing the ford.
When the air creaked, it was
A lapwing seeing us off the premises
Of its private marsh. A snuffling puff
Ten yards from the boat was the tide blocking,
Unblocking a hole in a rock.
When the black drums rolled, it was water
Falling sixty feet into itself.

When the door
Scraped shut, it was the end
Of all the sounds there are.

You left me
Beside the quietest fire in the world.

I thought I was hurt in my pride only,
Forgetting that,
When you plunge your hand in freezing water,
You feel
A bangle of ice round your wrist
Before the whole hand goes numb.

IN MY MIND

I go back ways to hurl rooftops
into that furze-blazing sunset.

I stare at water
frilling a stone, flexing a muscle.

Down sidestreets I sniff
cats in passages, old soup and

in one hot room
the fierce smell of hyacinths.

From the tops of spires
I lasso two counties in one eye-blink

and break my ears with a jukebox
in a frowsy cellar.

I am an honorary citizen
of these landscapes and a City Father

of this city. I walk
through its walls and burn

as traffic lights. It is all
lines on my hand.

But I turn away
from that terrible cul de sac.

I turn away from
that terrible cul de sac

and the room in it
with green blinds drawn

and a bed with a bed lamp shedding
its kind light down

on a dead hand
and a book fallen from it.

MILNE'S BAR

Cigarette smoke floated
in an Eastern way
a yard above the slopped tables.

The solid man thought
nothing could hurt him
as long as he didn't show it—

A stoicism of a kind. I
was inclined to agree with him,
having had a classical education.

142

To prove it, he went on telling
of terrible things that had
happened to him—

so boringly, my mind
skipped away among the glasses
and floated, in an Eastern way,

a yard above the slopped
table; when it looked down,
the solid man

was crying into his own mouth.
I caught sight of myself
in a mirror

and stared, rather admiring
the look of suffering
in my middle-aged eyes.

MIRROR

My thought, poor abstract, caresses that richer one,
The idea of you. I sit in a cold sun

And there's their image, lamenting on its own—
Lubricious water wooing a cold stone.

VISITING HOUR

The hospital smell

combs my nostrils
as they go bobbing along
green and yellow corridors.

What seems a corpse
is trundled into a lift and vanishes
heavenward.

I will not feel, I will not
feel, until
I have to.

Nurses walk lightly, swiftly,
here and up and down and there,
their slender waists miraculously
carrying their burden
of so much pain, so
many deaths, their eyes
still clear after
so many farewells.

Ward 7. She lies
in a white cave of forgetfulness.
A withered hand
trembles on its stalk. Eyes move
behind eyelids too heavy
to raise. Into an arm wasted
of colour a glass fang is fixed,
not guzzling but giving.
And between her and me
distance shrinks till there is none left
but the distance of pain that neither she nor I
can cross.

She smiles a little at this
black figure in her white cave
who clumsily rises

in the round swimming waves of a bell
and dizzily goes off, growing fainter,
not smaller, leaving behind only
books that will not be read
and fruitless fruits.

WRITERS' CONFERENCE, LONG ISLAND UNIVERSITY

The moderator's spectacles twinkle in the light.
His brain twinkles in five languages.
Two speakers sit on each side of him, desperately
at ease. The microphone
sucks his words in and sprays them
out again over the dry
audience. All round and overhead, glitters
a poor man's Sistine Chapel
of gold scrolls and foiled trumpets, of
pumped-up Cupids and Muses, their blank eyes
unable to show
the astonishment they're unable to feel
at the languages of the world
crackling and sibilating around them
instead of
what they were used to—the revolving orbs
of Eddie Cantor, Ethel Merman's Guinness and
velvet voice—hoofers and clowns and galvanised
tap-dancers—all gone, all gone,
now fat in penthouses or mad
in flophouses or
silent at last under the sibilating
language of grass.

The panel, tails feathering, give tongue after
an elusive quarry. But

145

no votes will be taken. No
resolution will be made.—That
will be left to the grass
that counts no votes but by which
a resolution will be passed that
no-one will contradict
in any language.

But the quarry will not
stop running. And the sweet vocables
will carry their human thoughts in pursuit of it
into territories where,
though the quarry always escapes,
new thoughts will meet them and new worlds
seem possible.

NO CHOICE

I think about you
in as many ways as rain comes.

(I am growing, as I get older,
to hate metaphors—their exactness
and their inadequacy.)

Sometimes these thoughts are
a moistness, hardly falling, than which
nothing is more gentle:
sometimes, a rattling shower, a
bustling Spring-cleaning of the mind:
sometimes, a drowning downpour.

I am growing, as I get older,
to hate metaphor,
to love gentleness,
to fear downpours.

THE ROSS-SHIRE HILLS

What are the hills of Ross-shire like?
Listen. I'll tell you. Over the snow one day
I went out with my gun. A hare popped up
On a hill-top not very far away.

I shot it at once. It came rolling down
And round it as it came a snowball grew,
Which, when I kicked it open, held not one
But seventeen hares. Believe me or not. It's true.

FACING THE CHAIR

Here under the rays of the sun
Where everything grows so vividly
In the human mind and in the heart,
Love, life, and all else so beautifully,
I think again of men as innocent as I am
Pent in a cold unjust walk between steel bars,
Their trousers slit for the electrodes
And their hair cut for the cap
Because of the unconcern of men and women,
Respectable and respected and professedly Christian,
Idle-busy among the flowers of their gardens here
Under the gay-tipped rays of the sun.
And I am suddenly completely bereft
Of *la grande amitié des choses créés*,
The unity of life which can only be forged by love

A CHANGE OF WEATHER
February 1966

Even the cauld draps o' dew that hing
Hauf-melted on the beard o' the thistle this February day
Hae something genial and refreshin' aboot them
And the sun, strugglin' airgh and wan i' the lift,
Hauf-smoored in the grey mist, seems nane the less
    An emblem o' the guid cause.

It's like quality in weather, affectin' a'thing
But aye eludin' touch, sicht, and soond,
Naething o' the Earth sinks deeper noo
Aneth the canny surface o' the mind
Than autumn leaves driftin' on a lochan.

Yet thinkin' o' Scotland syne 's like lookin'
Into real deep water whaur the depth
Becomes sae great it seems to move and swell
Withoot the slightest ripple, yet somehoo gie's me
An unco sense o' the sun's stability
And fills me, slowly, wi' a new ardour and elasticity.

It's like having—hashish, is it?

airgh—reluctant; *lift*—sky; *hauf-smoored*—half-smothered; *guid*—good;
a'thing—everything; *aneth*—beneath; *lochan*—small lake; *syne*—then;
gie's—gives; *unco*—strange.

THE BOG IN SPRING

Here in the evening an artist would find inspiration
For the trick of evolving colour in shadow
—Producing colour for the sake of light
Rather than light for the sake of colour.
For the colours of Spring's livery are not emphatic,
Unlike those of winter and summer, here,
But more toned, far subtler in the blending,
Baffling in their quick transitions from saffron to silver,
And from silver-grey to white when the eveining "sokes"
Steal up the "deeks." Clumps of reeds waving, dark-brown
      tassels
And green-blue rises of marshland suddenly
Become spectacular with the magic touch of Spring's sun
Just as when artfully coloured lights are cast
On a theatre's bits of symbolic scenery.
This is the charm of the bog in Spring—
The sudden emergence of the landscape with vital colour.
Only yesterday the scent was but a poor shrivelled composi-
      tion
—The reed-beds a dead-wood colour as if left over
From last year. To-day the process of a new birth 's
      complete.
The slow river and meandering waterways move
With the mysterious throb of life. The forlorn marsh farm,
Starkly rectangular to the eye, is now
Peeping transfigured from some proscenium
Of alder and sallow.—Summer's herald 's trumpeting.
O look! O look! Two or three days ago
There was nothing but formless wastes
Of yellow reed and slate-blue waters
Gleaming flatly beneath the hard March sunshine.

The yellow has turned to a pale amber now,
The water is a silvery-grey,
And a vague wreath of mist hangs over the lush grassland
Giving the illusion of immense translucent distances.
The air is heavier, as if awaiting with more certain
        expectancy
The unmistakable voice of early Summer.

The empty sky of March is replaced by a sky
Full of light and faery shapes, feathery clouds
Floating or drifting lazily, enchanting
The somewhat mournful tranquillity of the soft grey wastes
        of the lagoon.
Now you can hear the earliest short sleepy-like croak
Of the erstwhile torpid frogs. They hop from their holes
Feeling their way into the warming waters, influenced
By the thrill of the universal burgeoning of Spring.
They'll come out in platoons to-morrow, shiny, black-
        stained,
Growing ever more venturesome until at night
If you go down to the 'deeks' you'll hear
Their quaint orchestration, their croaking Serbonian lullaby,
Down below in the very bowels of the marsh.

ALASTAIR MACKIE b. 1925

IN THE PARK

The trees are lanesome; it maun be a' the steer
o' fowk streekit oot ower this aifterneen
fu' o' cast claes and cares, a' the human gear
like eerands opened oot to passin' een.

The feedin' o' five thoosan' on ice-cream;

and kittled wi' the band's stramash o' brass
that snores and cuitters to them in their dream
when "It's the pipers. Gie them room to pass."

Like a hangin'. Whit swung i' the simmer lift
they couldna say, but the skirl o the air 's
gane clean thro' them like the pint o' a dirk

and they've fa'n gey quait. They didna shift
but bade to see them linkin' oot in pairs
and when they stoppit they deed wi' a yerk.

lanesome—lonely; *maun*—must; *steer*—commotion; *fowk*—people; *streek-it*—stretched; *aifterneen*—afternoon; *fu'*—full; *claes*—clothes; *eerands*—purchases; *een*—eyes; *kittled*—tickled; *stramash*—uproar; talks low; *simmer lift*—summer sky; *skirl*—shrill sound; *pint*—point; *dirk*—dagger; *fa'n*—fallen; *gey quait*—very quiet; *bade*—remained; *linkin'*—walking briskly; *deed*—died; *yerk*—jerk.

STILL LIFE—CÉZANNE

They bide still, but it was a sair fecht
atween them baith. The white claith wid aye jist
cowp doun like a lynn aneth the aipples' wecht.
It haed to be like the sinens o' 's fist.

And the aipples! Yon was mason's wark.
They shogged thegither like cramasy bells
till they cam doun to the grun' wi' a yark.
He hauds them there till the colour mells

and makes them, 'oor by 'oor, as on the tree.
Drap-ripe they fa' the wecht o' a muckle stane
intill his hands, and wi' a gey dour grace

as tho' they grippit something his wersh ee
haed ettled to haud and tak for his ain,
and they daurna', for yon glower on his face.

bide—stay; *sair fecht*—sore fight; *atween*—between; *baith*—both; *claith*—
cloth; *aye*—always; *cowp*—tumble; *lynn*—waterfall; *aneth*—beneath;
wecht—weight; *sinens*—sinews; *shogged*—shook; *thegither*—together;
cramasy—crimson; *yark*—heavy blow; *hauds*—holds; *mells*—mixes; *'oor*
—hour; *wersh*—raw; *ettled*—attempted; *ain*—own; *daurna*—daren't;
glower—scowl.

SCHOOLQUINE

I mind ye when your hair was straucht
a lassie like the lave,
till ae day, sudden-like, ye lookt up
oot o' blue een,
sma' white fingers roond the bowl o' your face
and I thocht syne in the blink o' an ee
your ain een tellt me whit the glees lang kent
when ye gied yoursel' at nicht
and the haill room was quait,
blate and fearfu' like the beats o' your hert,
and ye saw syne your briests burgeonin'
and your body cam hame to ye wi' a saft lowe
ye cairry still the wey ye haud your heid
and your narra' fingers crook aboot your lips.

Nae quine but queen.
I stand and watch ye gang your wey
aneth the douce airches o' your poo'er.
The loons glower at your by-gaein
tint awhile as the lowe nods.

schoolquine—schoolgirl; *straucht*—straight; *lave*—remainder; *ae*—one;
glees—sideways looks; *kent*—knew; *gied*—gave; *haill*—whole; *blate*—
shy; *syne*—then; *lowe*—flame; *douce airches*—gentle arches; *poo'er*—
power; *loons*—boys; *glower*—stare; *by-gaein*—passing by; *tint*—lost; *nods*
—sleeps.

VOX HUMANA

The marled earth tyaaves roon in space
Gey trauchelt wi the muckle wecht
O' seas and continents and men.
But gin ye listen a while—what then?
Yon sound that trimmles through the gird o space
Is nae the axial grind, nor the pech o gravity
But you and me and the haill human race.

Pascal was feart o the star-sawn silence,
But mair fearfu than aa yon
Is the lang lamentations o human kind
Baith yirth and starns are deef til.
Like a cairn it spiels unseen
Intil the birl o toom and ootlan warlds
Up til the Empyrean.
And never the din dwines awa.

Wha hearkens til 't?
Whaur 's the Columbus o a thoosand and one starns
That sall hing his flags on the skerries o oor wrangs
And pint us tae salvatioun?
Whaur 's the great Captain wi een like gless
That strides alang the planets like a causey,
His hands fu o gauds and a new deliverance?
Nane hear it but we oorsels.

The cairn we bigg, we alane maun brak
Or brak oorsels, and mak the earth lichter
Wi oor deaths, than wi oor lives.

marled—variegated; *tyaaves*—struggles; *trauchelt*—troubled; *muckle wecht*—great weight; *gin*—if; *trimmles*—trembles; *gird*—hoop; *girn*—snarl; *pech*—pant; *haill*—whole; *feart*—afraid; *yirth*—earth; *starns*—stars; *deef*—deaf; *spiels*—climbs; *birl*—whirl; *toom*—empty; *ootlan*—outlandish; *causey*—road; *gauds*—toys; *bigg*—build; *maun brak*—must break; *lichter*—lighter.

ALASDAIR MACLEAN b. 1926

QUESTION AND ANSWER

"Do you love me? Do you love me?"
You keep on repeating the question.
"Say you love me. I want to hear you say it."
I say that once, when I was very young,
I saw a rat caught in a trap,
in a wire cage, squealing and snapping.
The cage was lowered into a tank of water.
It watched the stream of bubbles
slacken and at long last cease,
and when the cage was raised to the surface
the dead rat clung to the roof,
its jaws so firmly clamped around the wire
they had to be chiselled free.
But all this I say to myself;
to you I mouth, sullenly but truthfully,
the words you want to hear.
Satisfied then, you turn your back for sleep
and I lie awake, feeling the taste of the wire
between my teeth, feeling, in the darkness,
the cold water flow over me.

A TEST OF ALONENESS

Not simply when you are minus people.
That can be borne.
But when you sit in your room and listen
to the nitrogen bubbles forming in your blood.
When you stick your hand in the refrigerator
and something pulls you in.
When you're afraid to take a bath
in case the water turns crimson.
When every third or fourth or fifth lamppost
is more important than the rest.
When all the doors loom like tunnels.
When the traffic hurtles past you
at a hundred miles an hour.
When your tongue keeps swelling
in the middle of a sentence.
Most of all, when the person
who goes always with you, unseen by others
—your one companion—
begins to walk a little apart from you,
begins to shrug and wink and tap his forehead.

THE ROAR

". . . . it would be like hearing the grass grow and the squirrel's
heart beat, and we should die of that roar which lies on the other
side of silence."—George Eliot.

Beyond silence you would find a more contingent world.
Your breath would hang about you like a hurricane.

155

A signal gun would boom every second from the castle
of your heart. You would dream in the surf of your blood.

Your peeled nerves would curl to the scream of cut flowers,
to yesterday's conversations, to the clatter of falling snow.

Whispers grown muscular would make a trampoline of you,
bouncing with manic violence, beating you into the ground.

On that other scale bass notes would fracture glasses
and new high notes would rip your flesh like buzz saws.

With all the pillows ever made piled on your weary head
there would be no sleep for you. Your eyes would atrophy.

You would be a radio telescope, tuned in on Creation.
You would be God's dog, transfixed by your Master's whistle.

VISITING HOUR

He comes on, speaking almost as
convincingly as when his speech was new.
She fluffs her lines. Doped to the eyes
she waits for a more urgent cue.

Pain rouses her at last, uncurling in
her womb and kicking with both feet.
Her body arches, bridging life and death.
Her fingers pluck the sheet,

while his, ugly with nicotine,
shred the doorway's automatic stub.
Held half against his will he speculates
upon the nearness of the nearest pub.

That's answerable, at least. But this?
Beyond this evil any good?
His friends, who fear the venom of his tongue,
would neutralise with a platitude.

"That's life, old chap. How did the poet put it?"
"We all must in the earth be equal laid?"
He nods his thanks to such, reminded
that there will have to be arrangements made.

One could, of course, anticipate the end
by pinching out this light, now growing dim.
Would that be love, or self-love, though? Meanwhile
the screens around her bed encircle him.

SORLEY MACLEAN b. 1911

CURAIDHEAN

Chan fhaca mi Lannes aig Ratasbon
No MacGill–Fhinnein aig Allt Eire
No Gill-Iosa aig Cuil-Lodair,
Ach chunnaic mi Sasunnach 'san Eiphit.

Fear beag truagh le gruaidhean pluiceach
Is glùinean a' bleith a chéile,
Aodann guireanach gun tlachd ann—
Comhdach an spioraid bu tréine.

Cha robh buaidh air " 'san tigh-òsda
'N am nan dòrn a bhith 'gan dùnadh,"
Ach leóghann e ri uchd a' chatha,
Anns na frasan guineach mùgach.

Thàinig uair-san leis na sligean,
Leis na spealgan-iaruinn beàrnach,
Anns an toit is anns an lasair,
Ann an crith is maoim na h-àraich.

Thàinig fios dha 'san fhrois pheileir
E bhith gu spreigearra 'na dhiùlnach:
Is b'e sin e fhad 's a mhair e,
Ach, cha b' fhada fhuair e dh' ùine.

Chum e ghunnachan ris na tancan,
A' bocail le sgriach shracaidh stàirnich
Gus an d' fhuair e fhéin mu 'n stamaig
An deannal ud a chuir ri làr e,
Bial sìos an gainmhich 's an greabhal,
Gun diog o ghuth caol grànnda.

Cha do chuireadh crois no meadal
Ri uchd no ainm no g' a chàirdean:
Cha robh a bheag dhe fhòirne maireann,
'S nan robh cha bhiodh am facal làidir;
'S có dhiùbh, ma sheasas ursann-chatha
Leagar móran air a thàilleabh
Gun dùil ri cliù, nach iarr am meadal
No cop sam-bith a bial na h-àraich.

Chunnaic mi gaisgeach mór á Sasuinn,
Fearachan bochd nach laigheadh sùil air;
Cha b' Alasdair a Gleanna Garadh—
Is thug e gal beag air mo shùilean.

HEROES

I did not see Lannes at Ratisbon nor MacLennan at Auldearn nor Gillies (MacCain) at Culloden, but I saw an Englishman in Egypt.

A poor little chap with chubby cheeks and knees grinding each other, pimply unattractive face—garment of the bravest spirit.

He was not a hit "in the pub in the time of the fists being closed," but a lion against the breast of battle, in the morose wounding showers.

His hour came with the shells, with the notched iron splinters, in the smoke and flame, in the shaking and terror of the battlefield.

Word came to him in the bullet shower that he should be a hero briskly, and he was that while he lasted, but it wasn't much time he got.

He kept his guns to the tanks, bucking with tearing crashing screech, until he himself got, about the stomach, that biff that put him to the ground, mouth down in sand and gravel, without a chirp from his ugly high-pitched voice.

No cross or medal was put to his chest or to his name or to his family; there were not many of his troop alive, and if there were their word would not be strong. And at any rate, if a battle post stands many are knocked down because of him, not expecting fame, not wanting a medal or any froth from the mouth of the field of slaughter.

I saw a great warrior of England, a poor manikin on whom no eye would rest; no Alasdair of Glen Garry; and he took a little weeping to my eyes.

EADH IS FÉIN IS SÀR-FHÉIN

Chaidh na samhlaidhean leis a' bhearradh
Agus na h-ìomhaighean thar na creige
Is chailleadh iad air machair fharsaing
Air cabhsair an rathaid dhìrich
O'm faic an reusan an fhìrinn.

Chan eil a' mhachair idir farsaing
Agus tha an rathad lùbach
Is ged a tha sgurrachan a' bhearraidh
Corrach do threibhdireas an t'-seallaidh,
Chan fheàrr a' choille throm dhùmhail
'S i fàs a mach a cnàimh an rathaid,
As mo chluasan, as mo shùilean,
As mo bhial, as mo chuinnlein
'S as gach bìdeig de m' chraiceann,
Eadhon as an roinn bhig sin
A tha blàth os cionn mo chridhe.

Tha imcheist na machrach móire
Cho doirbh ri sgurrachan na dórainn.
Chan eil buaidh air a' mhachair
's chan eil bhith beò anns a' choille.

Chan fhuirich an cridhe air a' mhachair;
'S mór as fheàrr leis a' chridhe
('s e cho càirdeach do 'n spiorad)
Bhith 'n crochadh air piotan ris an stalla

Is fear mór 'na cheannard ròpa,
Calvin no Pàp no Lenin
No eadhon bragairneach bréige,
Nietzsche, Napoleon, Ceusair.

Tha Freud 'na bhàillidh air a' choille
(Tha 'n oifis aige àrd air uirigh)
'S air gach oighreachd nach tuigear.
Cha mhoth' airsan fear an ròpa
(An ròp e fhéin 'na bhalg-séididh);
Sùil saoi air friamhaichean céine;
Uirigh 'san chreig chais uaibhrich
A' toirt neor-thaing do choille 'n luasgain,
Do 'n choille fhìrinnich ìochdraich,
Do 'n choille iriosail 's i air laomadh
Le luibhean searbha dathte mìlse.

ID, EGO AND SUPER-EGO

The symbols went over the escarpment and the images over the cliff and they were lost on a wide plain, on the causeway of the straight road from which reason sees the truth.

The plain is not at all wide and the road is twisty, and though the peaks of the escarpment are unsteady for sincerity of vision, the thick heavy wood is no better, growing out of the bone of the road, out of my ears, out of my eyes, out of my mouth, out of my nostrils, and out of every little bit of my skin, even out of that little part that is warm above my heart.

The perplexity of the great plain is as difficult as the peaks of grief. The plain has no grace and there is no living in the wood.

The heart, which is such a close relative of the spirit, will not wait on the plain; it much prefers to hang from a piton against the rock face with a big man as rope-leader, Calvin or Pope or Lenin, or even a lying braggart, Nietzche, Napoleon or Kaiser.

Freud is factor of the woodland (his office is high on a ledge) and of every incomprehensible estate. He doesn't much regard the ropesman (the rope itself a bellows); sage eye on distant roots, (his) ledge in the steep proud rock defying the restless wood, the truthful subject wood, the humble wood that teems with bitter variegated sweet plants.

CÓIG BLIADHNA FICHEAD O RICHMOND
1965

Ag gabhail sìos troimh Shasuinn
Air an t-slighe luaith
Chunnaic mi comharradh ceann-rathaid
Gu Richmond air Suail.

Chuimhnich mi bòidhche a' bhaile
'S e 'g éirigh 'na shràidean casa
le cabhsairean cloiche cruinne,
Mar bha 'san stàbull 's a' Chlachan;
Lùb na h-aibhne 's an t'-seann abaid,
An LEÓGHANN DHUBH 's an LEÓGHANN ÒIR,
Leathad uaine 's an t-seann eaglais.
Cha robh móran ann a chòrr
Ach saighdearan air na sràidean,
Saighdearan 's na LEÓGHAINN ag òl:
Sasunnaich, Albannaich, Cuimrich;
Móran ag giùlan an cuid dragha
Agus a' mhór-chuid socair laghach.

Cha robh móran a bharrachd
Na mo chuimhne ach an Caisteal.

O chionn cóig bliadhna fichead
Mi fhìn liom fhìn anns a' Chaisteal
A' dol timchioll liom fhìn;
Cha b' ann a dheanamh sgrùdaidh
Air seann togail no seann dìon,
Ach a' sgrìobadh m' eanchainn 's mo chridhe
Fiach an beirinn air aon dòigh
Air fuasgladh na teanchrach do-labhairt
A ghreimich coibhneas agus gaol,
Onair tuigse agus feòil.

Cha b' e an caothach brùideil Nàsach
No daorsa thruagh na Frainge
A dhùin an teanchair air mo chridhe
Ach diol-déirce bochd mnatha
A rùisg dhomh annas giar a cràdhloit,
Do nach robh agam ri thairgsinn
Ach faileas is farainm a' ghaoil
—Is iarmailt reultach fhaoin nan dàn
A chuireadh sgleò air a càs—
A chionn 's nach robh 'na colainn bhreòite
Thioram mhillte an treòir sin
A riaraicheadh neart na h-òige.

Ann an aonaranachd a' Chaisteil
Dhaingnich mi mo chiad bhòid
—A thug mi bliadhna roimhe sin—
Bòid uasal uaibhreach na h-Ìobairt
A shàsaich fearas-mhór mo shìnnsre:
Agus bha 'n seann chaisteal làidir
'Na ìomhaigh air anabarr an àrdain
Bu bhaideal air anabarr mo ghaoil.

O chionn cóig bliadhna fichead

Cha do shaoil mi, 's beag bha dh' fhios a'm
Gum fàsadh uabhar cridhe 's cainnte
O ghòraiche na h-òinnsich meallta
'S i cur an treabhaidh bhuirb neònaich
Troimh thobraichean na glaine còire,
'S ag cur mathachaidh nach do shaoil sinn
Air bàrr trom a readh gu laomadh.

'S beag bha dh' fhios a'm air a cràdhlot:
Nach robh ann ach seòrsa diachainn
A thig a adhaltranas 's a briagan.

'S fhad on dh' ionnsaich mi a chaochladh,
Le peileirean, mèinean, sligean aognaidh,
Le bristeadh buaidhe is eu-dòchas,
Le gort an spioraid is n feòla:
Gur miosa na suarachas òinnsich
An samh a seòmar-gas na h-Eòrpa.

Ma théid mi lath-eigin a Richmond
'S gum faic mi 'n Caisteal cuimir làidir,
Cha toir e orm ach snodha-gàire
Mas cuimhne liom idir mo chràdhlot.

TWENTY-FIVE YEARS FROM RICHMOND
1965

Going down through England on the fast way, I saw a road-end
sign to Richmond on Swale.

I remembered the beauty of the town rising in steep streets with
cobbles like those in the stable in Clachan; the bend of the river
and the old abbey, the Black Lion and the Golden Lion, a green
slope and the old Church. There wasn't much more but soldiers

on the streets, soldiers drinking in the Lions: Englishmen, Scots-
men, Welshmen; many bearing their own tributes and the
majority nice and good-natured.

There wasn't much more in my memory but the Castle.

Twenty-five years ago myself alone in the Castle, going round
alone, not to examine old buildings or fortification but scraping
my brain and heart so that I might catch some way to loosen the
unspeakable vice that clamped kindness, love, honour, intellect
and flesh.

It was not the brutal Nazi madness nor the miserable slavery of
France that closed the vice on my heart but a poor object of
pity, a woman who had bared to me the sharp novelty of her
anguish, to whom I had to offer only the shadow and nickname
of love—and the starry vain firmament of the poems that would
put a film over her case—since there was not in her hurt dry
spoiled body the vigour that would satisfy the strength of young
manhood.

In the loneliness of the Castle I confirmed my first vow—which
I had taken a year before—the generous proud vow of sacrifice,
which satisfied the uppishness of my ancestry: and the strong
old castle was an image of the excess of the hauteur that was a
battlement on the excess of my love.

Twenty-five years ago I did not think, little did I know that pride
of heart and language would increase from the folly of the silly
deceitful woman, who was putting a barbarous strange
ploughing through generously clean wells and who was putting
a manure we did not realise on a heavy crop that would go to
seed.

Little did I know of her sore wound: that it was only a kind of
trial that comes from adultery and lies.

I have long since learned the opposite, with bullets, mines,
deathly shells, with defeat in victory and despair, with famine
of the spirit and of the flesh: that worse than the baseness of a
silly woman is the stench from the gas-chamber of Europe.

If I go someday to Richmond and see the shapely strong Castle,
it will only make me smile if I remember my agony at all.

JOSEPH MACLEOD b. 1902

FLORENCE: SLEEPING IN FOG

Our olives safe from mildew
slumber towards sweet oil.
Cats and cars in stall
and our children snug.
In a basket a convex dog.

But round the house it clams,
the halitosis of old water,
round and over the home,
a moulding, a suppurating,
subsisting return of flood.

TO AN UNBORN CHILD

Whichever you are, woman or man, whoever you are
already you are,
five months shaping, to shape and be shaped by
the shapes of your world.

We of the world can show you the contours only,
never the footsteps.
Already your way of walking has curdled in you.

You may greet the year 2000, may
tour the moon, or find God, may
measure thought, or merely live, you
gathering of beauty, you
handful of giant, and nobody like you
before or to come, you
one new space-spot of continuing eternity
in the womb of love.

But whatever you may be signalling already
from your wired brain to flickering life,
kicking, thrusting, to be our daughter, our
son, my formed hand feels you and futures you
furth of the fluid rampart
fluid into the fluidity of our world,
which we did not make,
but did not succeed in remaking.

WILLIAM MONTGOMERIE b. 1904

TRIPTYCH OF MINIATURES

I.

TO THE DARK LADY OF THIS SONNET

Let me go then into those dark flowers
fall in long parabolas through black skies
over continents sliding to dawn and sunset
symbols of a world I hold in my hands and kiss

or in those dark eyes tunnel the Alps
from green Swiss valleys to long fields
in Lombardy   walk *nella Loggia della Signoria*
or Magna Graecia's temples with red oleanders.

But thin nebulae under dark eyelashes
are mist on white peaks in high passes
drifting over ricefields among windbreak
saplings shivering over frozen ditches.

The nebulae would flash jale gold ulfire
to stars did I know the word spoken in the beginning.

II.

AUTOLYCUS TO MEROPE

To-night this lift with automatic mind
counts 1 to 10
                    10 to 1
zero
        Sisyphus counts his ten fingers
or heaves his eternal punishment to the tenth floor.

Hermes my father taught me metamorphosis
I shall shape-shift you to Merope the Pleiad
Long ago the lift-man forgot you
his simple brain is wired to an electric main.

Shall we leave his lift or walk downstairs
unconsidered moments stolen from time
away from the taped music and chatter in the bar
long enough to say I love the laughter in your eyes?

Later between two dances shall we look at Orion
(framed in the window) chasing your six sisters?

III.

Do I dare disturb the universe?

I put a night square of darkness from Pegasus
in the typewriter
                              tap diamond Sirius
Mars the ruby
                    Vesper silver goddess
symbols of a mathematic beyond Einstein.

Slipping the Great Dog I flush Capricornus
along a short-cut goatpath
that telescopes the universe to a yardstick
of space-time
                    a starred ellwand.

That jewelled ell of three stars
is a child's ruler to measure infinities of indifference.
I chuck it back into the dark attic of the sky
I'd rather trust my hand holding your hand
eyes your eyes
                    ears your voice
                                        until
in these three jewels I understand *you*.

EDWIN MORGAN b. 1920

ONE CIGARETTE

No smoke without you, my fire.

169

After you left,
your cigarette glowed on in my ashtray
and sent up a long thread of such quiet grey
I smiled to wonder who would believe its signal
of so much love. One cigarette
in the non-smoker's tray.
As the last spire
trembles up, a sudden draught
blows it winding into my face.
Is it smell, is it taste?
You are here again, and I am drunk on your tobacco lips.
Out with the light.
Let the smoke lie back in the dark.
Till I hear the very ash
sigh down among the flowers of brass
I'll breathe, and long past midnight, your last kiss.

FRONTIER STORY

Meanwhile, back at the ranch factory
they were turning out whole stampedes
just for the hell of it, the mile-long door slid back
and they reverted to dust at the first touch of air.
But the music of the dust flowed back over the assembly-line
and that was the Christmas of a thousand million cowboys.

Steers went lowing upland, purple sage country
with boots on marched west out back as
bulldozers like mobile capital cities
trunched up dead million-bed motels and charged
some gaily eroded buttes with simulating cowboys.

The diggers were worse than any sands of the sea
and dynamite only loosened myriads off sideways

till a bag of megatons went critical and
there were horses' eyeholes all over the Coalsack
and when we came in we were crunching through cowboys.

Or so we were told as we laid Los Angeles on Boston
and took a few states out, we were only playing,
pulled Mexico up over us and went to sleep,
woke up spitting out Phoenicians into the Cassiterides
and gave a yawn a wave as it flew out full of cowboys.

They sat in our teeth with red-hot spurs and I said
"Back to the drawing-board," but the belt was humming
and pushed the continuum into funky gopher-holes
with a prime number down each hole wheezing
so cheekily we had to make more cowboys

first. Meanwhile, back at the ranch
factory they were diligently making
us, just for the hell of it, the mile-long door
slid back and we reverted to dust at the touch
of air. But our music lingers in the bones of cowboys.

CANEDOLIA
an off-concrete scotch fantasia

oa! hoy! awe! ba! mey!

who saw?
rhu saw rum. garve saw smoo. nigg saw tain. lairg saw lagg.
rigg saw eigg. largs saw haggs. tongue saw luss. mull saw yell.
stoer saw strone. drem saw muck. gask saw noss. unst saw cults.
echt saw banff. weem saw wick. trool saw twatt.

how far?
from largo to lunga from joppa to skibo from ratho to shona
from ulva to minto from tinto to tolsta from soutra to marsco
from braco to barra from alva to stobo from fogo to fada from
gigha to gogo from kelso to stroma from hirta to spango.

what is it like there?
och it's freuchie, it's faifley, it's wamphray, it's frandy, it's
sliddery.

what do you do?
we foindle and fungle, we bonkle and meigle and maxpoffle. we
scotstarvit, armit, wormit, and even wifflet. we play at crosstobs,
leuchars, gorbals and finfan. we scavaig, and there's aye a bit of
tilquhilly. if it's wet, treshnish and mishnish.

what is the best of the country?
blinkbonny! airgold! thundergay!

and the worst?
scrishven, shiskine, scrabster, and snizort.

listen! what's that?
catacol and wauchope, never heed them

tell us about last night
well, we had a wee ferintosh and we lay on the quiraing. it was
pure strontian!

but who was there?
petermoidart and craigenkenneth and cambusputtock and
ecclemuchty and corriehulish and balladolly and altnacanny
and clauchanvrechan and stronachlochan and auchenlachar and
tighnacrankie and tilliebruaich and killieharra and invervannach
and achnatudlem and machrishellach and inchtamurchan and
auchterfechan and kinlochculter and ardnawhallie and inver-
shuggle

172

and what was the toast?
schiehallion! schiehallion! schiehallion!

GLASGOW GREEN

Clammy midnight, moonless mist.
A cigarette glows and fades on a cough.
Meth-men mutter on benches,
pawed by river fog. Monteith Row
sweats coldly, crumbles, dies
slowly. All shadows are alive.
Somewhere a shout's forced out—"No!"—
it leads to nothing but silence,
except the whisper of the grass
and the other whispers that fill the shadows.

"What d'ye mean see me again?
D'ye think I came here jist for that?
I'm no finished with you yet.
I can get the boys t'ye, they're no that faur away.
You wouldny like that eh? Look there's no two ways aboot it.
Christ but I'm gaun to have you Mac
if it takes all night, turn over you bastard
turn over, I'll—"

                                    Cut the scene.
Here there's no crying for help,
it must be acted out, again, again.
This is not the delicate nightmare
you carry to the point of fear
and wake from, it is life, the sweat
is real, the wrestling under a bush
is real, the dirty starless river
is the real Clyde, with a dishrag dawn

173

it rinses the horrors of the night
but cannot make them clean,
though washing blows
                        where the women watch
by day,
            and children run,
                        on Glasgow Green.

And how shall these men live?
Providence, watch them go!
Watch them love, and watch them die!
How shall the race be served?
It shall be served by anguish
as well as by children at play.
It shall be served by loneliness
as well as by family love.
It shall be served by hunter and hunted in their endless chain
as well as by those who turn back the sheets in peace.
The thorn in the flesh!
Providence, water it!
Do you think it is not watered?
Do you think it is not planted?
Do you think there is not a seed of the thorn
as there is also a harvest of the thorn?
Man, take in that harvest!
Help that tree to bear its fruit!
Water the wilderness, walk there, reclaim it!
Reclaim, regain, renew! Fill the barns and vats!

Longing,
            longing
                        shall find its wine.

Let the women sit in the Green
and rock their prams as the sheets
blow and whip in the sunlight.
But the beds of married love
are islands in a sea of desire.

Its waves break here, in this park,
splashing the flesh as it trembles
like driftwood through the dark.

THE STARLINGS IN GEORGE SQUARE

I.

Sundown on the high stonefields!
The darkening roofscape stirs—
thick—alive with starlings
gathered singing in the square—
like a shower of arrows they cross
the flash of a western window,
they bead the wires with jet,
they nestle preening by the lamps
and shine, sidling by the lamps
and sing, shining, they stir
the homeward hurrying crowds.
A man looks up and points
smiling to his son beside him
wide-eyed at the clamour on those cliffs—
it sinks, shrills out in waves,
levels to a happy murmur,
scatters in swooping arcs,
a stab of confused sweetness
that pierces the boy like a story,
a story more than a song.
He will never forget that evening,
the silhouette of the roofs,
the starlings by the lamps.

II.

The City Chambers are hopping mad.

Councillors with rubber plugs in their ears!
Secretaries closing windows!
Window-cleaners want protection and danger money.
The Lord Provost can't hear herself think, man.
What's that?
Lord Provost, can't hear herself think.

At the General Post Office
the clerks write Three Pounds Starling in the savings-books.
Each telephone-booth is like an aviary.
I tried to send a parcel to County Kerry but—
The cables to Cairo got fankled, sir.
What's that?
I said the cables to Cairo got fankled.

And as for the City Information Bureau—
I'm sorry I can't quite chirrup did you twit—
No I wanted to twee but perhaps you can't cheep—
Would you try once again, that's better, I—sweet—
When's the last boat to Milngavie? Tweet?
What's that?
I said when's the last boat to Milngavie?

III.

There is nothing for it now but scaffolding:
clamp it together, send for the bird-men,
Scarecrow Strip for the window-ledge landings.
Cameron's Repellent on the overhead wires.
Armour our pediments against eavesdroppers.
This is a human outpost. Save our statues.
Send back the jungle. And think of the joke:
as it says in the papers, It is very comical
to watch them alight on the plastic rollers
and take a tumble. So it doesn't kill them?
All right, so who's complaining? This isn't Peking

where they shoot the sparrows for hygiene and cash.
So we're all humanitarians, locked in our cliff-dwellings
encased in our repellent, guano-free and guilt-free.
The Lord Provost sings in her marble hacienda.
The Postmaster-General licks an audible stamp.
Sir Walter is vexed that his column 's deserted.
I wonder if we really deserve starlings?
There is something to be said for these joyous messengers
that we repel in our indignant orderliness.
They lift up the eyes, they lighten the heart,
and some day we'll decipher that sweet frenzied whistling
as they wheel and settle along our hard roofs
and take those grey buttresses for home.
One thing we know they say, after their fashion.
They like the warm cliffs of man.

FROM THE DOMAIN OF ARNHEIM

And so that all these ages, these years
we cast behind us, like the smoke-clouds
dragged back into vacancy when the rocket springs—

The domain of Arnheim was all snow, but we were there.
We saw a yellow light thrown on the icefield
from the huts by the pines, and laughter came up
floating from a white corrie
miles away, clearly.
We moved on down, arm in arm.
I know you would have thought it was a dream
but we were there. And those were trumpets—
tremendous round the rocks—
while they were burning fires of trash and mammoths' bones.
They sang naked, and kissed in the smoke.
A child, or one of their animals, was crying.

Young men blew the ice crystals off their drums.
We came down among them, but of course
they could see nothing, on their time-scale.
Yet they sensed us, stopped, looked up—even into our eyes.
To them we were a displacement of the air,
a sudden chill, yet we had no power
over their fear. If one of them had been dying
he would have died. The crying
came from one just born: that was the cause
of the song. We saw it now. What had we stopped
but joy?
I know you felt
the same dismay, you gripped my arm, they were waiting
for what they knew of us to pass.
A sweating trumpeter took
a brand from the fire with a shout and threw it
where our bodies would have been—
we felt nothing but his courage.
And so they would deal with every imagined power
seen or unseen.
There are no gods in the domain of Arnheim.

We signalled to the ship; got back;
our lives and days returned to us, but
haunted by deeper souvenirs than any rocks or seeds.
From time the souvenirs are deeds.

SUMMER HAIKU

Pool.
Peopl
 e plop!
Cool.

178

WAVES

w a v e r i n g   w a y f a r i n g

w a v i n g

w a f e r y   w a v y

w a v i n g

w a i f

w a v i n g

From BOATS AND PLACES

I.

row the sea
row it easy
Rothesay

II.

Greek
       creek
creak
caïque

BRAINCHILD

Finally, nerve-ending to nerve-ending
in shiny synthetic sheaths,
they completed the transplant
and left the theatre exhausted, triumphant,
and god-like. All white coats and teeth
they laughed at the photographer, all nine,
but for an anxious second each felt like Frankenstein.

The little fellow grew up
puzzled that someone else's memory
should distort his view, a puppet
jerking on its knotted strings,
programmed by reverberating rings
of neurones not his own.

Sometimes he suffered phantom pain
for a lost soul, saw alarming visions,
heard devils and angels sing;
then suddenly one black day
his hand came to its own decision
and blew out someone else's brain.

NIGG

Time alone separates the dull red
Granite of these cliffs and the red
Clay in the kirkyard yonder.
As I stand on this grey day,

With scarce a breath to sunder
The wetness of air and sea,
Let my living and my dead
Surround me. Let them say
Who carried the sea upon his back,
What fish sucked the marrow from whose bones,
Drifting like the untidy sea-wrack,
Whose blood seeps now to colour the clay
Of the ploughed field and the crimson cliff.

I would have written an epitaph
To please them and to honour the good,
The mortal drudgery, the valour
That lie now beneath the cold wet gravestones.
But the whistling peewit mocks my mood.
And anyway they would not have understood.

THERE IN THE MIRROR

There in the mirror I glimpse him,
dark smoothly-parted hair,
cheeks red and shaved with care
and an open razor; brushed and dressed
in black camphorated Sunday best;
a big man.
                    Rough clothes put away—
no salty oilskin chafes the neck—
he exchanges tarry deck
for polished pew on Sabbath day.

Protected from high living
by Presbyterianism and poverty,
on pleasures of the flesh a ban,
yet joyful in his love of God and man,

he died, the cancer at his breast,
wasted, yellow and agonised.
My faith not his was lost.

I circle buzzing razor round
my cheeks, haloing father which art
(seconds only have unwound
since I stared into the mirror-ground)
in heaven. I shiver to see pent
anguished and uninnocent
a stranger in his place—
my own Sunday face.

DAVID MORRISON b. 1941

DANCE, GLENNA

Dance, Glenna, for my blood
Is thin with the weather,
And coldness catches the nerve.

Old men with their last coals
Huddle round the fire,
Chatting, chittering.

Their minds and eyes are tired
With the world and its users.

Dance for them, Glenna,
And their wives who have forgotten
How once they could dance.

Dance for children,
So that they can envy

And wish one day to be you.

Dance for me, Glenna;
This winter night needs the spark
Of your eye and foot.

And dance for yourself, Glenna,
For lately you have talked
Of growing old.

THE ROOT

You cut the root o the tree
And left tae dee, that flower
Sae reid and fresh,
A sang witherin wi the sun.

Petals crack i the haun,
And ashes lie aneath
Branches that sheltered the yerd,
Where roots aince twined.

Aye, you cut the root o the tree
And left tae dee, a sang
Tae ma hauchlin hert,
A sang weel sung.

You cut the root o the tree.

dee—die; *haun*—hand; *aneath*—beneath; *yerd*—earth; *aince*—once; *hauch-lin*—limping.

STEPHEN MULRINE b. 1938

WOMAN'S COMPLAINT

If, husband, I should say,
    "A young man looked at me today,
    took pleasure in my lower lip,
    knelt down in fabled sand to clip
    me naked in his arms," would it surprise
you? Yet he did, and in his eyes
I might have played oblivious, desired
his delta fingers to enrich my tired
hair, his drying mouth to crush
my matronly objections. But the blush
I cost him turning snapped the spell,
and in its spread I watched him tell
my years. And though we shared,
husband, nothing else, that moment stared
us down, to years, to unkept rage.
And if I were to say, husband, "Age
    does not creep up on a woman; decay
    is an instant discerned in the play
    of young hunger and young self-respect
    over faded erotica," would it affect
you? Would you write sonnets, fight duels, deny that I'm old?
Or does all this leave you, as me, mortally cold?

THE COMING OF THE WEE MALKIES

Whit'll ye dae when the wee Malkies come,
if they dreep doon affy the wash-hoose dyke
an' pit the hems oan the sterrheid light,

an' play keepie-up oan the clean close-wa',
an' blooter yir windae in wi' the ba',
missis, whit'll ye dae?

Whit'll ye dae when the wee Malkies come,
if they chap yir door an' choke the drain,
an' caw the feet frae yir sapsy wean,
an' tummle thur wulkies through yir sheets,
an' tim thur ashes oot in the street,
missis, whit'll ye dae?

Whit'll ye dae when the wee Malkies come,
if they chuck thur screwtaps doon the pan,
an' stick the heid oan the sanit'ry man;
when ye hear thum come shauchlin' doon yir loaby,
chantin', "Wee Malkies! The gemme's . . . a bogey!"
haw, missis, whit'll ye dae?

whit'll—what will; *dae*—do; *dreep*—drip; *affy*—off; *dyke*—wall; *pit*—put;
oan—on; *sterrheid*—stairhead; *close-wa'*—wall of the entrance-corridor;
blooter—smash; *chap*—knock at; *caw*—knock; *sapsy wean*—simpleton
child; *wulkies*—acrobatics; *tim*—empty; *screwtaps*—beer-bottles; *schauch-
lin'*—shuffling; *loaby*—lobby; *the gemme's a bogey*—the game is a devil
(war-cry).

ALAN RIDDELL b. 1926

BOULDERS UNDERWATER

From a height, and on days of no wind,
boulders on the bed of a bay look like
bubbles held down there by the great pressure above them.
Rounded by time and the ocean, and even more
rounded by the burring optic of water, they lie,
pressed together, herded almost, in a deep

hug of silence.

Imagine, then, what a strange chorus of sound
any afternoon might burst forth from the sea if only
that muffling weight were lifted and they all
floated innocently up to the surface.

THE WINDOW

Opening a window onto trees and hills you see
(among tall trees and hills and set in stone)
a window opening onto where you know
you never were or could have been and there,
walking through sunlit forests, people go
waving their arms like underwater fronds
you cannot grasp however much you try,
with pale aquarium eyes dilating at
the shadows falling on them laughing now
deep in that baffling landscape, till you pull
the window to and, turning round, reveal
the charred and gutted ruins smoking still.

FAILED-SAFE
deterrent
err
terre
rent

women
o
   men
wo e
  omen

BREAKDOWN

from the heart to
the blood from the
blood to the brain
from the brain to
the blow from the
blow to the blast
from the blast to
the bridge from the
bridge to the pledge
from the pledge to
the plague from the
plague to the plea
from the plea to
the hope from the
hope to the hurt
from the hurt to
the heart from the
heart to the blood
from the blood to
the brain from the
brain to the brain
to the brain to
the brain to the

ON THE EMBANKMENT
(For Hugh MacDiarmid)

These Embankment afternoons,
heavy with nostalgia,
stir memories of action
in the antique frigates laid-up for display,
and, to come nearer the point,
rub more than the sea's salt
into my own momentarily forgotten wounds.

Yet the situation is not without its humour,
knowing one has a full belly and almost enough
money to pay the rent for a year should that often written
    about
worst come to the worst
(Quite a change from the old times!)
Yes, not without humour, knowing one has after all—
even if ingloriously—
somehow managed to survive.
The really depressing thought of course is the waste :
the slow disintegration of the personality consistent
failure seems to leave in its wake.
And not just the artistic
failure, or the 'ill-starred' essays into the greater
romanticism of love, but also the simple
failures of communication between
relatives and friends, and the inability
to derive interest or sustenance from
the bread-and-butter labours each and all of us
necessarily have to endure.

As if, in itself, experience were not sufficient :
increasing awareness, for once, unable to sustain
the precarious balance between knowledge and
    affirmation;

resulting, as it were, in a kind of
emotional hysterisis; the heart lagging behind
the mind's bloody but perceptible advances.

Which is why to-day, in this alien environment,
and between jobs, I think of you,
Chris, and your bulldozing progress
through the debris of these years, and marvel at
the extraordinary resilience of your spirit, as freshly alive,
now as thirty years ago, to the essentially human
nature of the problems which underlie
the major political and social upheavals of our time, as to
the subtle gradations of colour which transform
the tawny surface of a Scottish bog in Springtime
into a shimmering carpet of unbelievable iridescence.

OLD ADAGE

crawl before you
walk before you
run before you
creep

R. CROMBIE SAUNDERS b. 1914

INTERRUPTIONS

The little girl opened her hand
and fourteen flamingoes flew into the air—
she saw them.

O trumpets and gay ophicleides!
When will your melodious march be equalled?
I walked under the trees with a book
opened at page
eleven,
it was about aero-dynamics
a subject in which I take a moderate interest

but the little girl opened her hand
and fourteen flamingoes flew into the air

IMPERFECT

I love you so much
I cannot love you at all

The emperor's garden
was famous for its roses
but two of the beds
were marred by inferior blooms.
The great stag shot on Tuesday
was a fifteen pointer, which meant
eight tines on one antler, only
seven on the other

I love you so much
I cannot love you at all

DERELICT COTTAGE

You've seen so many like it : the door gone

Long since to make a fire or mend a barrow,
The room where earwigs scutter over fragments
Of window glass, bones of small birds, sheep droppings.

"Haunted," they say. An easy explanation
Of the distress that makes a man aware
(Finding perhaps among the ancient nettles
A doll's head that affection once had fleshed

But blind and brainless in the summer air)
That it's not people do the haunting here,
Rather the purpose of forgotten lives

That lingers in a valley children played in
And Sandwood Bay, a socket in a skull,
Left sightless at the edge of the Atlantic.

ALEXANDER SCOTT b. 1920

BALLADE OF BEAUTIES

Miss Israel Nineteen-Sixty-Eight is new,
A fresh-poured form her swimsuit moulds to sleekness,
Legs long, breasts high, the shoulders firm and true,
The waist a lily-wand without a weakness,
The hair, *en brosse* and black, is shorn to bleakness,
Yet shines as stars can make the midnight do—
But still my mind recalls more maiden meekness,
Miss Warsaw Ghetto Nineteen-Forty-Two.

Her masters filmed her kneeling stripped to sue
The mercy barred as mere unmanning weakness,
Or raking rubbish-dumps for crusts to chew,
Or licking boots to prove her slavish meekness,

Or baring loins to lie beneath the bleakness
Of conquerors' lust (and forced to smile it through),
Her starving flesh a spoil preferred to sleekness,
Miss Warsaw Ghetto Nineteen-Forty-Two.

The prize she won was given not to few
But countless thousands, paid the price of meekness,
And paid in full, with far too high a due,
By sadist dreams transformed to functioned sleekness,
A pervert prophet's weakling hate of weakness
Constructing a mad machine that seized and slew,
The grave her last reward, the final bleakness,
Miss Warsaw Ghetto Nineteen-Forty-Two.

Princesses, pale in death or sunned in sleekness,
I dedicate these loving lines to you,
Miss Israel Sixty-Eight and (murdered meekness)
Miss Warsaw Ghetto Nineteen-Forty-Two.

TO MOURN JAYNE MANSFIELD
(Decapitated in a car crash, June 1967)

I.

SAIR SONNET

Cauld is thon corp that fleered sae muckle heat,
Thae Babylon breists that gart the bishops ban
And aa the teeny titties grain and greet
That siccan sichts should gawp the ee o man.

Still are the hurdies steered sic houghmagandie,
The hips sae swack, their ilka step a swee,
That graybeards maun hae risen hauflin-randie

192

To merk them move and move the yirth agee.

Faan is thon powe that crouned her fairheid's flouer,
Hackit awa as gin by the heidsman's aix—
Our lust the blade has killed thon bonnie hure,
Puir quine! that aince had reigned the Queen o Glaiks.

Owre aa the warld the standards canna stand,
Wauchied their strength as onie willow-wand.

II.

HOLLYWOOD IN HADES

Jayne Mansfield, strippit mortal stark
    O' aa her orra duddies—
For thae that sail in Charon's barque
    Keep nocht aside their bodies—
Comes dandily daffan til Hades' dark,
    A sicht to connach studies.

Yet Pluto, coorse as King Farouk,
    Gies only ae bit glower—
She's naukit, ilka sonsie neuk,
    But he's seen aa afore—
And turns to tell the t'ither spook,
    "Marilyn, move outowre!"

cauld—cold; corp—body; muckle—much; gart—made; ban—curse; teeny
titties—small young girls; grain and greet—groan and weep; siccan sichts
—such sights; gawp—gape; ee—eye; hurdies—buttocks; steered sic hough-
magandie—stirred such fornication; swack—supple; swee—sway; maun—
must; hauflin-randie—lustful as adolescents; yirth—earth; agee—off
balance; faan—fallen; powe—head; fairheid—beauty; gin—if; heidsman—
executioner; thon bonnie hure, puir quine—that lovely whore, poor girl;
glaiks—good-for-nothings, optical illusions; wauchied—enfeebled; mortal—
exceedingly; orra duddies—worthless rags; dandily daffan—sporting like a
spoiled woman; connach—destroy; ae bit glower—one brief scowl; naukit

193

—naked; *ilka sonsie neuk*—every comely corner; *t'ither*—other; *outowre*
—out over.

SABBATH

"Come unto me, all ye that are heavy-laden"—

The portly paunches trundled
the few short steps (O merciful religion!)
from the car to the door of the kirk,
the loaded furs lurching
from limousines to cushioned pews—

Pagan, I paused,
the Sunday papers under my infidel arm,
amazed at the joyful vision of
gentle Jesus
kicking camel-fat backsides
through a needle's eye.

DOUN WI DIRT!

"De Sade?"
"Ach, gyaad!"

"Masoch?"
"Eh, fyauch!"

"Frank Harris?"
"Guid war us!"

"Jim Joyce?"
"Nae choice!"

"Bert Lawrence?"
"Abhorrrrence!"

"Hank Miller?"
"Wud spiller!"

"Jean Genet?"
"Och, dinnae!"

"Bill Burroughs?"
"Gomorrah's!"

"Syd Smith?"
"Deil's kith!"

"Al Trocchi?"
"Fell mochie!"

"Al Sharp?"
"Coorse carp!"

"The bourach?"
"Just smoorich!"

"Mankind?"
"Muck-mind!"

"And you?"
"Weel, nou—"

gyaad, fyauch—expressions of disgust; *guid war us*—God defend us; *wud spiller*—mad destroyer; *dinnae*—don't; *deil's kith*—devil's acquaintance; *fell mochie*—extraordinarily putrescent; *coorse carp*—coarse talk; *bourach* —heap; *smoorich*—a big wet kiss.

LANDFALL

The great ship gently riding a sea of stars,
We slipped from frozen sleep
To the warm wonder of waking's dawn
From a night ten thousand centuries dark,
And knew we neared our far galactic harbour
(Haven for humankind)
Undrowsing engines sought for through our dreams
And homed upon with heartless hope for hearts.

The sphere we saw come breasting a spume of stars,
Swimming to save us,
Raft among all the rocks of ruined systems,
Reefs of burned-out suns,
A second earth, a globe whose untouched glory
Glowed in the solar light,
A dazzle of ocean, luminous green of land,
And pearled by long combs of cloud.

Rocketting down from the sterile-splendid stars,
We watched the apple under us swell and swell
To a green gourd,
To a round meadow,
A mazy map of mingled shine and shade.

We strangers out of the stars,
Orphaned from Earth, made waifs to wander
Space and its thronging void
For one new womb that seed of man might quicken,
For one new hearth where hands could kindle fire,
For one new home to wear the shapes of loving,
For one new land to carry all our crosses,
For one new world to sign with work and wounds—
Suddenly knew it, suddenly named it ours.

Dearer than stars,
More deeply known for sorrow
And known for love,
For love of life, for life,
For all our lives, for all the lives before us,
We knew it, suddenly,
Suddenly,
Knew it the mother of man
And knew it the mistress mine of all his making.

Through all the stars
We fled among for refuge, searching, seeking
The secret Eden,
The planet of quiet joys,
The raging Earth left silenced by space and sleep,
The ship unsleeping slid
Through troughs of time
And crests of rough creation
To find us the fitting scene for sons of men,
One world in all the worlds whose clouded skies
Would rain their blessings blissful on hearts unblest,
Whose fields would feed our fruitless hunger,
Whose rivers slake the thirst no water quenches,
Whose seas would drown our grief,
The ship with mindless patience filing away all failures
Sought still for still success,
Went circling over the arc of all the systems,
Curved through the constellations,
Rounded the zodiac's zone,
And wakened us watching
Our newfoundworld.

Stripped of men for the stars,
Its wilderness shone for us to garden,
And every peak the Ararat of
        EARTH.

WEST GOING WEST?

from missal
to missile

SUMMARY

The Lord commanded humankind,
Increase and multiply.

But the people
Grew and divided.

TOP OF THE POPS

Lowpers, gowpers,
Duntily dowpers.

Skirlers, dirlers,
Bumpily birlers.

Yowlers, growlers,
Sappily sowlers.

Ravers, clavers,
Hotchily havers.

Jiggers, figures,
Trippily triggers.

Beggars, fleggers,
Langily leggers.

Yarkers, warkers,
Stoundily starkers.

Maeners, grainers,
Lowdenly laners.

Daters, maters,
Neibourly naiturs.

Craiturs, craiturs.

Leapers, gapers, possessors of throbbing backsides. Screamers,
thrillers, bumping whirlers. Howlers, growlers, simpleton souls.
Ravers, gossipers, jerking chatterers. Dancers, figures, tripping
neat ones. Beggars, swingers, the lengthily-legged. Quick movers,
workers, gleefully thrilling nudes. Moaners, groaners, awed
loners. Daters, maters, neighbourly natures. Creatures for whom
we feel affection repeatedly.

MARILYN MONROE STILL, 1968

The substance grins from a skull, the shadow smiles,
The flesh that has long wept from the bones
Glows on the page with a paradise glory,
Immortally golden,
Her sensuous sainthood haloed
By shining sex
That makes her yet the all too mortal world's
Miraculous maiden.

Her beauty's flame

Was fed by the forced draught
That howled from despair,
The emptiness inmost, gibbering void
Of bastard ancestral voices
Denying identity, sneering at sense of self,
Insisting on naked negation,
The falseness of fortune, that fickleness fame,
The uttermost absence of love
For lust's madonna
Shrined in a hell of proxied passions
Where fornicators spat our fantasies
To foul her image.

Those hatreds hurricaned,
Blew out her blaze
With brutal breath.

SPEIRIN

What wey? The cry
Gaes skirlan by
Yearhunder eftir hunder,
But nane can hain
What scaurs o stane
Cry back frae far owre yonder,
The sound gets drouned
Afore its wound
Can stob the hert o wonder.

What wey? We pry
In thon maist high
And maist unfaddomed ferlie,
The weird owre feared
That finds us sweird

To thole sae lang and sairly,
          But tak the lack
          O' answer back
Frae speirin late and early.

speirin—asking; *what wey*—why; *gaes skirlan by*—goes screaming past; *yearhunder eftir hunder*—century after century; *nane*—none; *hain*—preserve from harm; *scaurs*—cliffs; *stob*—pierce; *unfaddomed ferlie*—unfathomed marvel; *weird*—fate; *sweird*—reluctant; *thole*—endure.

CRY

Breakdown, breakdown, lay me low,
I'll go where all the furies go,
Into my own Orestian heart,
And tear it apart, tear it apart,

Breakdown, breakdown, hoist me high,
I'll fly where all the vultures fly,
Into my own Orphean brain,
And pick it clean, pick it clean.

Breakdown, breakdown, drive me deep,
I'll creep where all the blindworms creep,
Into my own Tiresian blood,
And drink its flood, drink its flood.

Breakdown, breakdown, pay me peace,
I'll cease where all the madmen cease,
Inside my own Oedipan mind,
And brand it blind, brand it blind.

KISSAN KATE

O maistress mine,
My cutty quine,
The sun himsel 's your lover,
He waps ye roun
Frae cuit til croun,
A kissan-closest cover.

But eftir dark
He tines his spark,
Anither love is lowean,
I wap ye ticht
In nearest nicht—
It's aa the warld I'm rowean.

The warld o you
I haud in lieu
O' Earth that sunlicht stories,
My hert wi yours
Ayont his pouers
In midnicht's glamour o glories.

cutty quine—small girl; *waps*—wraps; *cuit til croun*—ankle to crown;
eftir—after; *tines*—loses; *lowean*—blazing; *rowean*—wrapping up; *ayont*
—beyond; *glamour*—magic.

EIGHTEEN

Plucking songs from the air,
Seventeen poems in seven days,
And all winners,
I think of a six-year silence,

Six winter trees
With not a single bird—

And meantime
I net the eighteenth lark.

TOM SCOTT b. 1918

AULD SANCT-AUNDRIANS—BRAND THE BUILDER

On winter days, about the gloamin hour,
Whan the knock on the college touer
Is chappan lowsin-time,
And ilk mason packs his mell and tools awa
Ablow his banker, and bien forenenst the waa
The labourer haps the lave o the lime
Wi soppan secks, to keep it frae a frost, or faa
o suddent snaw
Duran the nicht,
And scrawnie craws flap in the shell-green licht
Towards you bane-bare rickle o trees
That heeze
Up on the knowe abuin the toun,
And the red goun
Is happan mony a student frae the snell nor-easter,
Malcolm Brand, the maister,
Seean the last hand throu the yett
Afore he bars and padlocks it,
Taks ae look round his stourie yaird
Whaur chunks o stane are liggan
Like the ruins o some auld-farrant bigging:
Picks a skelf out o his baerd,
Scliffs his tacketty buits, and syne
Clunters hamelins doun the wyn'.

Alang the shore,
The greinan white sea-owsen ramp and roar.
The main street echoes back his clinkan fuit-faas
Frae its waas,
Whaur owre the kerb and causeys yellow licht
Presses back the mirk nicht
As shop-fronts flude the pavin-stanes in places,
Like the peintit faces
Whures pit on, or actresses—ay, or meenisters—
To plaese their several customers.
But aye the nordren nicht, cauld as rumour,
Taks command,
Chills the toun wi his militarie humour,
And plots his map of starns wi deadly hand.

Doun by the sea,
Murns the white snaw owre the rack ayebydanlie.

Stoupan thro the anvil pend
Gaes Brand,
And owre the coort wi the twa-three partan creels,
The birss air fu
o the smell of the sea, and fish, and meltit glue,
Draws up at his door, and syne,
Hawkan his craig afore he gangs in ben,
Gies a bit scrape at the grater wi his heels.

The kail-pat on the hob is hotteran fu
o the usual hash o Irish stew,
And by the grate, a red-haired bewtie frettit thin,
his wife is kaain a spurtle round.
He swaps his buits for his baffies but a sound.
The twa-three bairnies ken to mak nae din
Whan faither's in,
And sit on creepies round about.
Brand gies a muckle yawn, and howks his paper out.

Tither side the fire,
The kettle sings like a telephone wire.

"Lord, for what we are about to receive
Help us to be truly thankful—Aimen—
Wuman, ye've pit ingans in 't again."

"Gae wa ye coorse auld hypocrite!
Thank the Lord for your maet, syne grue at it!"

Wi chowks drawn ticht in a speakless sconner
He glowers on her:
Syne on the quate and straucht-faced bairns:
Faulds his paper doun by his eatin-airns,
And, til the loud tick-tockin o the knock,
Sups, and reads wi nae ither word nor look.

The warld outside,
Like a lug-held sea-shell, roars wi the rinnan tide.

The supper owre, Brands redds up for the nicht.
Aiblins there's a schedule for to price,
Or somethin nice
On at the picters—sacont hoose—
Or some poleetical meetin wants his licht,
Or aiblins, wi him t-total aa his life,
No able to seek the pub to flee the wife,
Daunders out the West Sands "on the loose."
Whatever tis,
The waater slorps frae his elbucks as he synds his phiz.

And this is aa the life he kens there is.

gloamin—twilight; knock—clock; chappan lowsin-time—striking the time
to stop work; ilk—each; mell—mason's mallet; ablow—below; banker—
hewing table; bien forenenst the waa—snug against the wall; haps the
lave—cover the remainder; rickle—sketetal collection; heeze—rise; knowe

knoll; *snell*—bitter; *yett*—gate; *stourie yaird*—dusty yard; *liggan*—lying;
auld-farrant biggin—old-fashioned building; *skelf*—splinter; *scliffs*—scuffs;
tacketty buits—nailed boots; *syne*—then; *clunters hamelins*—moves
heavily homewards; *wyn'*—lane; *greinan*—yearning; *owsen*—oxen; *fuit-
faas*—foot-falls; *causeys*—cobble-stones; *starns*—stars; *swaw*—wave;
wrack—seaweed; *ayebydanlie*—everlastingly; *pend*—arch leading to a
close; *partan creels*—baskets of crabs; *birss*—sharp; *fu*—full; *hawkan his
craig*—clearing his throat; *ben*—through; *kail-pat*—broth-pot; *kaain a
spurtle*—driving a wooden rod; *swaps*—exchanges; *baffies*—slippers; *but*—
without; *creepies*—stools; *howks*—digs; *tither*—the other; *ingans*—onions;
grue—take a disgust; *chowks*—cheeks; *sconner*—repulsion; *quate*—quiet;
eatin-airns—utensils; *lug*—ear; *redds*—tidies; *aiblins*—perhaps; *daunders*—
strolls; *slorps*—runs off; *elbucks*—elbows; *synds his phiz*—washes his face;
aa—all.

CURSUS MUNDI

(For R. Matheson)

For yae chiel up
There's ten are doun,
And for yae brim cup
There's ten that's toom;
As a miller's wheel
In a mill-race birled
Turns aye abreel,
Sae rowes this world.

Whaur ane hes ten
There's ten got ane
And a hunder men
That hevnae got nane;
Like a bairn's gird
Doun the Cougate dirled,
Wild owre the yird
Skelps on this world.

Thon landrowth man
Frae greed o gear
Gars his brither gan
In want and fear;
For a spadefü o glaur
His saul is nirled:
For better and waur
Sae rowts this world.

The rivers and lochs
Are claimed by Greed
As his proper auchts
Frae the fowk in need;
Ay, the welteran swaw,
Tho snarled and gurled,
He claims an' aa,
And the lave o this world.

Greed maks the law
That creates the crime,
And guid fowk aa
Are daean time;
As a fistfü o sand
In the wind's teeth hurled,
On the punishan hand
Blaws back this world.

Genius and sant
Rage out in pain,
And reformers rant,
But aa in vain;
As a carlin's shawl
Is plained and purled
Sae o dirt and saul
Plats up this world.

A cuif's preferred
Til a man o sperit,
And the faithless herd
Til ane o merit;
Like a prize bull
As dautit and curled,
The vainest fuil
Wins this world.

Wha shouts maist loud
Is heard the maist,
And wha maks maist gowd
Is deemit the best;
Like an auld duin bell
At a jee yett tirled,
Maugre hevin and hell
Jows on this world.

The glegger the shirker
The bigger his pey,
And the harder the worker
The sairer his wey;
Like a galley-slave
Til a lang-oar thirled,
Owre the buckeran wave
Kaas on this world.

Holy Will
Dreams up a kirk
To set himsel,
A lusty stirk;
Like an unholy tree,
Aa thrawn and knurled,
Throu scrabble and scree
Scoys up this world.

Sae psyche Dicks
Invent disease,
And their stigma sticks
On whaeer they please;
As a haill house faas
By white ants murled,
Thir termites' jaws
Knap doun this world.

Anxieties tak
Their toll o mense,
And on their rack
Ev'n a Burns tint sense;
As a deer in a baize
Owre a muir is whirled
On tapper taes,
Sae flees this world.

And Daeth in the end
Indifferently will
Gravewart send
Baith guid and ill;
Like a deid lament
On the gret pipe skirled,
Sic distinction shent,
Sae keens this world.

yae chiel—one fellow; *toom*—empty; *birled*—whirled; *abreel*—areel; *bairn's gird*—child's hoop; *dirled*—rattled; *yird*—earth; *skelps*—drives hard; *landrowth*—plentifully endowed with land; *glaur*—dirt; *nirled*—stunted; *waur*—worse; *rowts*—goes from place to place rummaging; *auchts*—possessions; *swaw*—wave; *snarled and gurled*—surly and growling; *lave*—remainder; *daean*—doing; *sant*—saint; *carlin*—old woman; *plats*—intertwines; *cuif*—simpleton; *dautit*—made much of; *duin*—worn out; *jee*—awry; *yett*—gate; *tirled*—rung; *maugre*—despite; *jows*—knells; *glegger*—slipperier; *sairer*—sorer; *thirled*—subjected; *buckeran*—awkwardly moving; *kaas*—drives; *stirk*—steer; *thrawn*—twisted; *knurled*—knobbly; *scrabble*—heather-stump; *scree*—débris on a mountainside; *scoys*—twists; *murled*—crumbled; *knap*—greedily eat; *mense*—decency; *tint*—lost; *baize*—hastening; *tapper taes*—tip-toes; *shent*—destroyed.

CHARLES SENIOR b. 1918

FULMARS

When it comes to sea cliffs
I am scared to go
too close to their edges,
the long drop below
would draw me down
from sheer pleasure of vertigo:
such fearful thrill
sucks like a groundswell
at the most thrawn will.

Trepidatious with ifs
I inch forward on wary toe
to see on sandstone ledges
unfledged chicks of artic snow,
lose my fear and frown
feasting eyes on feathered show,
for parent fulmars revel
in their winkle spiral
between foam and nesting sill.

TRIPTYCH

An icicle
that fuses water, light and air
within a blue acetylene flare
burns into a steady thaw
feeds back its substance
to the glare of melting snow

210

ignites softened memories
of foundering years;

a guttering candle
with blackhearted flame
has flounces of shadow
guarding the yellow blaze
and soon consumes
its own grey grief of tears;

while in the cave
a stalactite
luminous and bright with age
draws to a perfect point
from which its lactic
limestone drips to meet
and shape its opposite.

BURNS SINGER 1928-1964

BIRDSONG

The speck of protoplasm in a finch's egg,
—Watch it under its spotted shell—
It will one day be pinned upon a treetop
To curl the stresses of the straight blond breeze
With auburn musics, auspicious sunburnt notes
That are for me the triumph of the scenery.

Already, quietly, it winds temptations,
Harnesses the young blood

And bridles it with promises of discovery
To the delights which all the old ones know
Are, in success, as pointless as the breeze
Or these sharp spangles tramelling the wind's beak.

COMMUNITY OF WORSHIP

I believe in God.
It is not your God
Any more than it is my God.
It is not a member of the committees
That reflect international issues
While they perjure themselves with decisions.
It is not even
What goes on between us.
It is not
Kindness to the poor.
All these things are sometimes appropriate.
(Even I am sometimes appropriate
   And my God is not me.)
There are occasions—and you know them better than I do—
When loneliness is all that there is
And more than enough of it
Is enough.
There are dreams to which there is no admittance
—We all dream them.
There is a time which is secret.
Though only for us since the secret is
That there never was a secret between us.
But there is nothing
So difficult or so complete,
So hidden or so open,
So meaningless or so much the basis of meaning,
As the God we must both worship
Because there is no other.

HOME FROM SEA

The longest days are those spent at sea.
Waves dip heavily, trundling under our gunwale
An imagination or promise of the ocean as abyss.
The longest days are those we can hardly remember.
Dead waters retire. The smoke lingers unshaven
Or lounges from cabins into a corridor where
It collides helplessly with the stink of coffee.

There is no steadiness anywhere except in the arrival
Of another wave or another morning. The same
Unsteadiness, waves morning by morning,
Jolts without jest our neurotic banter.

Slowly around us the air circulates like
A paper that everyone has already re-read
And will re-read later. Ghostly
The engines clamber through the floor.

Cards collect grease from many fingers. Dust
Rubs along the ward-room to the galley.
The great sea collapses harmlessly outside
An unopening door.

Slipshod and sleepy, we calculate who we are.

We sit beside the clock that thuds so softly
Around its circles and dictates our duties.
Its monosyllables never threaten us.
We know we're safe; since, though the ocean flexes
Its watery muscles with a vast display,
There is inside those ships which sail the farthest
A shabby but invulnerable place that hedges
Stability with repetitive concision.

The clock, in monosyllables, repeats,
Time out of mind and out of time with ours,
A mile, a mile, another mile, until
One day it stops, neglected, unwound,
The current turned off : this is our destination.

A LANDSCAPED ROOM

Now that these threats
Like grey hairs
Hedge the sun's
Chubby brilliance,
Its boy's brash face
Discountenanced
By clouds and rains,
Two panes of glass
Shortsightedly
Glaze roughened stones,
The garden soil's
Moist breathing
Gathered outside.

"Keep distance out,"
The carpet cries.
A door dreams.
Walls sulk.
Warmth whispers
Threatened by mirrors.

But a discord
From overhead
Tumbles, trickles
And blackens the garden.
The greyhaired sun

Hears, as golden
Boys never can,
The patter of tears
In the deep distance.
An adult sun
Listens to trouble.
No answer is given.
The question rests.

The door crumples.
The carpet cries.
Stones return
The unbroken look
And distance sneers
At the room's two
Hollow eyes.

IAIN CRICHTON SMITH b. 1928

TWO GIRLS SINGING

It neither was the words nor yet the tune.
Any tune would have done and any words.
Any listener or no listener at all.

As nightingales in rocks or a child crooning
in its own world of strange awakening
or larks for no reason but themselves.

So on the bus through late November running
by yellow lights tormented, darkness falling,
the two girls sang for miles and miles together

and it wasn't the words or tune. It was the singing,
it was the human sweetness in that yellow,
the unpredicted voices of our kind.

OLD HIGHLAND LADY READING NEWSPAPER

Grasping the newspaper in kneaded hands
in her ordered bed, the tablets at the side,
she slowly reads of all her friends who've died
in the black holds of the approaching islands

where the horses and the daffodils are dead,
unfashionable skirts have swirled away
down the Dutch cornfields and the fields of hay
into the numerous caves of her bald head

bent over print and old remorseless hands
grasping these deaths, the tombstones all in white
her eyes traverse with gritty appetite
in the slow justice of her mouth's small sounds.

SCHOOLROOM

My room is bare and has no pictures in it,
not baldheaded Shakespeare nor grained Milton nor
any other dignitary or poet.

Because I suppose there's no virtue in a picture.
It's a disguise of what is really there,
a sort of lie. Milton might have approved.

But nevertheless the walls are very bare.
Should I disguise the cracks by some colour?
In "Samson Agonistes" this wasn't done.

But in point of fact the walls were all pulled down.
Even for children should I have stained glass windows?
Or pointless lions in a pointless desert?

Or is it egotism to offer only myself,
a resounding voice in a resounding room,
as Milton again in his own "Paradise Lost"?

ABERDEEN

Mica glittered from the white stone.
Town of the pure crystal,
I learnt Latin in your sparkling cage,
I loved your brilliant streets.

Places that have been good to us we love.
The rest we are resigned to.
The fishermen hung shining in their yellow
among university bells.

Green lawns and clinging ivy. Medieval
your comfortable lectures, your calm grammar.
The plate glass windows showed their necklaces
like writhing North Sea fish.

Nothing will die, even the lies we learn!
Union Street was an arrow
debouching on the crooked lanes, where women
sweated like leaking walls.

217

IN THE TIME OF THE USELESS PITY

In the time of the useless pity I turned away
from your luminous clock-face in the hopeless dark,
appealing to me greenly, appealing whitely.
Nothing I could do, I had tried everything,
lain flat on the rug, fluttered my spaniel paws,
offered you my house like an unlocked crystal—
and so it came, the time of the useless pity
when the roots had had enough of you, when they slept
elaborating themselves by themselves
when they shifted over from yours, seeking a place
different from yours to burst through and to pierce
with a royal purple, straight and delicate: sails
of the suave petals unfurling at the mast.

IN THE CAFE

The leaf-fringed fountain
with the grey Scots cherub
arches water
over the waterlogged pennies.

Mouths and moustaches move.
The sad-eyed waitress
hides her unringed hand.
Umbrellas stand at ease.

Outside, rain drips
soupily, "the soup of the day."
The sauce bottles are filled with old blood
above the off-white linen.

(Not that I didn't have
suitors, said the Edinburgh lady
seated in the shelter like a queen,
gloved hands on her own sceptre).

But the waitress meltingly watches
that white-haired three-year-old
a huge bubble with wicked teeth
combing his hair with his knife.

OLD WOMAN

Your thorned back
heavily under the creel
you steadily stamped the rising daffodil.

Your set mouth
forgives no-one, not even God's justice
perpetually drowning law with grace.

Your cold eyes
watched your drunken husband come
unsteadily from Sodom home.

Your grained hands
dandled full and sinful cradles.
You built for your children stone walls.

Your yellow hair
burned slowly in a scarf of grey
wildly falling like the mountain spray.

Finally you're alone
among the unforgiving brass,

the slow silences, the sinful glass.

Who never learned,
not even aging, to forgive
our poor journey and our common grave

while the free daffodils
wave in the valleys and on the hills
the deer look down with their instinctive skills,

and the huge sea
in which your brothers drowned sings slow
over the headland and the peevish crow.

MEETING

"They threw stones at me," the old man said.
"They were some pupils from your school."
I twitched with anger. What was I expected
to do for him, since I myself had cruel

intimations of mortality?
I almost turned away. He touched my coat.
"Sir!" he said. "Sir!" I whinnied at that cry.
An empty horror filled my throat.

Naked like a fine spiritual horse
jabbed by needles I turned back to him.
The mottled redness his intensely hoarse
words thrust from became almost dim

and slated with a lead servility.
His stick, thrust through that sunset, was on fire
with some dread question. I felt some pity

but more than pity a vain desire

for peace out of my precariousness.
"I'd know them." His obscene face writhed
with an agèd almost evil singleness.
Some helpless anger on my chest breathed

heavily. Why must it be like this,
this see-saw of the spirit. I turned away.
"I'll see," I said, "what can be done." His voice
droned slavishly. I hated him. The fray

to which he'd called me made me angry with him
I felt my fingers tighten round my case
because I hated him and because I came
into my weakness, hateful, ominous.

HIGHLAND PORTRAIT

Castles draw in their horns. The stones are streaming
with fine Highland rain. A woman's struggling
against the sour wet wind in a black skirt.
Mist on the mountains. Waterfalls are pouring
their tons of water with a hollow roaring.
The phantom chieftans pass the heavy port.

Fences straggle westwards. Absurd cattle
lift their shaggy heads through humming water.
A duck dives coolly into stylish seas.
Hotels are sleeping in their winter colours.
The oilskinned sailors wear their gleaming yellows.
Glencoes are wailing in the hollow trees.

Country of céilidhs and the delicate manners,

obstinate dowagers of emerald honours,
the rain has worn your metaphors away.
Only poor rays of similes are shining
from brooches and from buckles. The complaining
barren rocks and ravens fill the day.

Nothing to say except a world has ended.
The waters of Polldubh, direct and splendid,
will hump unsteady men to a boiling death.
Yet from the shaking bridge of fascination
we see in these the antiseptic passion
whose surgeon's reason is a kind of birth.

THA THU AIR AIGEANN M'INNTINN

Gun fhois dhomh tha thu air aigeann m'inntinn
mar fhear-tadhail grunnd na mara
le chlogaid 's a dhà shùil mhóir
's chan aithne dhomh ceart d'fhiamh no do dhòigh
an déidh cóig bliadhna shiantan
tìme dòrtadh eadar mise 's tu:

beanntan bùirn gun ainm a' dòrtadh
eadar mise 'gad shlaodadh air bòrd
's d'fhiamh 's do dhòighean 'nam làmhan fann.
Chaidh thu air chall
am measg lusan dìomhair a' ghrunna
anns an leth-sholus uaine gun ghràdh,

's chan éirich thu chaoidh air bhàrr cuain
a chaoidh 's mo làmhan a' slaodadh gun sgur
's chan aithne dhomh do shlighe idir,
thus' ann an leth-sholus do shuain
a' tathaich aigeann na mara gun tàmh
's mise slaodadh 's a' slaodadh air uachdar cuain.

YOU ARE AT THE BOTTOM OF MY MIND

Without my knowing it, you are at the bottom of my mind, like one who visits the bottom of the sea with his helmet and two great eyes: and I do not know properly your expression or your manner after five years of the showers of time pouring between you and me.
Nameless mountains of water pouring between me, hauling you on board, and your expression and manners in my weak hands. You went astray among the mysterious foliage of the sea-bottom in the green half-light without love.
And you will never rise to the surface of the sea, even though my hands should be ceaselessly hauling, and I do not know your way at all, you in the half-light of your sleep, haunting the bottom of the sea without ceasing and I hauling and hauling on the surface of the ocean.

A' DOL DHACHAIDH

Am màireach théid mi dhachaidh do m'eilean
a' fiachainn ri saoghal a chur an dìochuimhn'.
Togaidh mi dòrn de fhearann 'nam làmhan
no suidhidh mi air tulach inntinn
a' coimhead "a' bhuachaill aig an spréidh."

Dìridh (tha mi smaointinn) smeòrach.
Eiridh camhanaich no dhà.
Bidh bàt' 'na laighe ann an deàrrsadh
na gréin iarail: 's bùrn a' ruith
troimh shaoghal shamhlaidhean mo thùir.

Ach bidh mi smaointinn (dh'aindeoin sin)
air an teine mhór th' air cùl ar smuain,
Nagasàki 's Hiroshìma,
is ciuinnidh mi ann an rùm leam fhìn
taibhs' no dhà a' sìor-ghluasad,

taibhs' gach mearachd, taibhs' gach cionta,
taibhs' gach uair a ghabh mi seachad
air fear leòint' air rathad clachach,
taibhs' an neonitheachd a' sgrùdadh
mo sheòmar balbh le aodann céin,

gu'm bi an t-eilean mar an àirc
'g éirigh 's a' laighe air cuan mór
's gun fhios an till an calman tuilleadh
's daoine a' bruidhinn's a' bruidhinn ri chéile
's bogha-froise maitheanais 'nan deuran.

GOING HOME

Tomorrow I will go home to my island, trying to put a world
into forgetfulness. I will lift a fistful of earth in my hands or I
will sit on a hillock of the mind watching "the shepherd with his
sheep."

There will ascend (I presume) a thrush. A dawn or two will
rise. A boat will be lying in the glitter of the western sun and
water will be running through the world of the similes of my
intelligence. But I will be thinking (in spite of that) of the great
fire that is behind our thoughts, Nagasaki and Hiroshima, and I
will hear in a room by myself a ghost or two constantly moving.
The ghost of every error, the ghost of every guilt, the ghost of
each time I walked past the wounded man on the stony road,
the ghost of nothingness scrutinising my dumb room with distant
face, till the island is an ark rising and falling on a great sea and

224

no one knowing whether the dove will ever return, and people talking and talking to each other, and the rainbow of forgiveness in their tears.

POEM: "SOME MOVE OTHERS"

Some move others but themselves are stone.
Present them honour? No, present them none.
An alert coldness is to be despised
or let us praise the viper, the owl's eyes
globular in darkness, or the snow
that drifts forever on the world below.
Better the headlong soldier in his wrath
than the cool hand that plotted his hot graph,
O better in our vain and passionate wars
Love that moves the sun and the other stars.

THOSE WHO ACT

Those who act,

who bring the rope at the right time,

who know the kiss of life, have learnt
where the syringes and the drugs are,

Those who grow in the fact,

who see the stone in its perfect shadow
and do not ask why yellow is yellow,

To whom the car whirling in gravel
is that itself: and the will
itself, itself;

let these in their place be honoured
where the visible earth hangs on the cord

they pull: and light comes on.

TO HAVE FOUND ONE'S COUNTRY

To have found one's country
after a long journey
and it to be here
around one all the time.
It is like taking a girl
from the house next door,
after all that travel
that black dense wall.

To have fallen in love with
stone, thistle and strath,
to see the blood flow
in wandering old rivers,
this wound is not stanched
by handkerchiefs or verse.
This wound was after all
love and a deep curse.

Now I'm frightened to name it
lest some witch should spring

screaming out of the tombs
with a perverted broom.
I'm almost frightened to
name all the waters,
these seas, tall hills,
these misty bordered bibles.

Love's such a transient thing
except for that hard slogging
which, though it's love, we don't
name it by that ring
in which, tortured, we fight
with all the bones about us
in these cemeteries that hold
the feet in living grass.

SYDNEY GOODSIR SMITH b. 1915

LATE

Sweet hairt, I lay in bed last nicht
Alane and yet with ye
Alane I lay but no my lane
For the lane bed was full of ye.

Aa kens there's whiles a silly truth
Sets in the drunkard's ee—
Here nou 's a forest-bleezan truth
Frae the hairt o the barley bree:
Its flame inflames the tither flame
As ye, and me. . . .

We ken the flame inflames the flame
As the wind brings in the sea—
Ken, tae, that fire consumes itsel
    —As ye, and me.

hairt—heart; *my lane*—alone; *kens*—knows; *ee*—eye; *bleezan*—blazing; *barley bree*—whisky; *tither*—the other; *tae*—too.

THE KENLESS STRAND

My sails by tempest riven
The sea a race
Whaur suld be lown and lither
Aa's dispeace.

Dispeace o' hairt that visions
Reefs it downa ride,
Dispeace o' mind in rapids
Nane can guide:

And aye a face afore me
And anither face,
Ane luve's ancient tragedy
And ane its peace.

Here, on luve's fludetide I run
There, the unkent strand
Abune, the seamaws' tireless grief
Ayont, nae hyne, nae end.

riven—torn; *lown*—calm; *lither*—idleness; *aa*—all; *downa*—dare not; *ane*—one; *fludetide*—floodtide; *unkent strand*—unknown shore; *abune*—above; *seamaws*—seagulls; *ayont*—beyond; *hyne*—haven.

THREE
("Three men make a revolution."—Lenin.)

Wha 'd hae daith when there 's life?
Wha 'd tak a corpse in his teeth
When there 's live lips to pree?

Wha wad howk in moss or ice?
Wha 'd gie his life for anither
When there 's spital beds for free?

Wha, for grace, wad harp in Hevin?
Wha 'd haud the heid o' a deein dug
When Hevin has been delete?

Wha seeks a kenless fame herefter
—Men's memories and scholard's ink—
When nocht but here is ever?

Wha seeks eternity in a rotten flouer?
Wha racks the mountains faa like stour
When nane there 'll be to see it?

Wha 'd dae this and wha 'd dae yon
When end is nocht but naething?
You. Me. Anither.

---

wha 'd—who would; *hae*—have; *pree*—kiss; *howk*—dig; *gie*—give; *spital*
—hospital; *deein dug*—dying dog; *delete*—wiped out; *kenless*—boundless;
nocht—nought; *racks*—cares; *faa*—fall; *stour*—dust.

SPRING IN THE BOTANIC GARDENS

The trees are heavy with blossom—
And yet
As licht and lichtsome
As the birds that din,
Compete,
And fill all trees,
All licht,
With lustful chatter
Dartin, fidgin—
   For the ae live thing is livin.

Here I sit amang it aa,
Aa this blythful ignorance
—Or iggorant blythfulness—
Of lust and generation,
The sap and sang of protected things,
Sittin here in the park bink,
    Alane
        —yet no aa that alane.
The lovers airm in airm amang the trees
Bear seelie witness to a numen here:
All here is her and here she is allwhar—
But whar?
      Quick—look!
    Nane marks or mocks
    The viewless vision fleein by
    Naked white feet on the gress—
It was a dream of love, maybe,
The drowsy bard, rapt, in some ither
Paradiesgartlein.

What wad ye hae, then?
Misery? Joy?
There's millions stairvan owre the yerth,

There's thousands fechtin for nocht that they believe—
I sit here in peace.
A wee speug, fearless, pecks at my fuit.
Ah love, count thy blessings!
Ay—

But all's dependent on anither's strength.

licht—light; *fidgin*—moving restlessly; *ae*—one; *blythful*—merry; *bink*—bench; *seelie*—innocent; *allwhar*—everywhere; *fleein*—flying; *ither*—other; *yerth*—earth; *fechtin*—fighting; *wee speug*—tiny sparrow; *fuit*—foot.

I SAW THE MUNE

I saw the mune at nune the day
Blue sky and sun and the mune there tae
It was the morning and the evening baith thegither
It's aye the mornin and the eenin baith thegither

        —For us.

At the last day
As at the first.

    But this, hairtbeat,
    Is bang in the middle
    And wants nae bush—
    Nae mair nor gowden wine does
    Or a broch around the mune
                            That says
. . . . Rain. . . . rain. . . .

Rain, beat doun

231

And raise the gowden corn again;
Sun, sheen on, all orient,
First day and last;
Mune, sheen—
The mornin and the eenin baith thegither.

In the rule o' the sun brairs the corn,
Sweys in the souch o' the wind
Like the souch o' the swaw in the faur-aff sea,
The mune ascendant—
Her dominion there. . . . Selanna!

Venus. . . Ceres. . . . . Pluvius. . . .
    Names, juist names—
Sol and Luna there conjoined
    —Juist names.
        Names.

But though we name auld names, my maisters,
Calling the past to clout wir raggit coats
And decorate a platitude auld when God was a laddie,
Think nocht tis idle sherbet that we sup
In this Sicilian idolatrie—

Aa kens, nae need here to repeat,
There's millions on the earth has gods nor meat;
Thousands ligg in chains and need
For nocht but speakin freedom's leid.
In aa this waesomeness and want
Guilt for love were piddling cant.
Act, gin ye will, act and move!
But speak nae word except ye love
Or, humbug, let me see ye staund
And cast the first stane frae your haund.

Here we love, remote and safe,
And cry that love is unity—

Aa lovers think they hae it baith
Though the earth quags beneath their feet.

I saw the mune at nune the day,
Blue sky and sun—
A memorie.

mune—moon; nune—noon; the day—to-day; tae—too; baith thegither—
both together; nae mair—no more; gowden—golden; broch—halo; sheen
—shine; brairs—sprouts; sweys—sways; souch—sigh; swaw—wave; faur-
aff—far-off; wir—our; laddie—young boy; ligg—lie; leid—language;
waesomeness—woefulness; gin—if; quags—shakes like a quagmire.

NIGHT BEFORE, MORNING AFTER
(From *Kynd Kittock's Land*)

Ah, stay me wi flagons, dochter o' Sharon, comfort me,
Hain me, compass me about with aipples!
Cool this fevered spreit with seven-frondit docken,
Flagons, marjoram, green fields, Salome!
Belling beakers, let them be til my hand! Dance!
The corn be orient and immortal barley greit!
Stay me, shore me up thir rue-I-ends, ye cedars o' Lebanon!
    (Seceders o' Raasay, what say ye?)
Slocken my drouth with pippins, Hebe!
Rosemary, bed me, sort my place of biding, sain me,
Entreat me kindly, temper this tuneless carillon,
This cracked and untrue campanile, O Venezia, greenest isle!
    —Black Rose of Shalimar, white hands, come cherish me
And hap me haill, my soul, with hairtsome companie,
Licht unflichtering of this lichtless airt!
    Fetch tumblers, dear buffoons, carnalitie
And Mammon's blythsome Bridal-Sang. . . .
    —Venus Merrytricks, mix you the drinks!

233

Come, be merry, gintles, joy, carouse ye carefree
In the Creek of Darkness, laugh me revelry, lutes,
And all the royal piping of the west!
Haud and bind this boaster muckle-mou, and sing,
Sweet leddies; ay, discourse wi aa thy minstrelsie, my dear,
And let all pantomime be at my fee,
Cried the Great Auk in his munificence. . . . Ah, whit a man!
"On Tinto Tap there was a Cap"
But nou tis in my hand. . . . O slainte mhor, my happie
Hielandman frae outermaist bunds o Fife!
Och, cry a halt! Let's call the bummer's bluff
And drouth tak him that first cries Haud enuff!

*

But look, the dawn breaks sweetly white
Like a tired professional bride in Shangri-La
And gently, with insensible insistence
Says "All dune. Diversion ends,"
And pits a timeous closure to their fantasies.

For dawn is truth. The dawn is work.
The dawn is empty. Dawn is cauld and hard.
Maistly, though, the dawn is all her lane,
There's nane about but early slaves,
Lost lovers and broke drunks—

It was the dawin yesternicht
   (Gin ye see what I mean?)
Saumon-reid athort the eastern luift
And cauld as beggerie
As he daunert hame wi his sel, strayed reveller,
The drink in his kyte as deid and dune
As Cleopatra's chastitie
As a wedow-woman's vows o' constancie.

  Ay, it's been the lang nicht
  But the dawin it is in truth—and there's the sign,

Beyond aa naitural significatiouns, sir,
That gang aft agley, as ye ken:
Lo, there, Sanct Cuthbert's milk-cairts clopperin by,
Infallible, and the streetlamps
Deid asleep on their feet
As me on mine gey near,
He croons til his sel—maun get a shave,
Shape up—a drap o' the hair o' the Auld Kirk's dug
And we'se be as richt as rain—for a bit—
Maybe. Aurora shine on me. . . .

History sleeps nou, for a bittie.
Dreams and thochts and vain imaginings
Bow doun wi a lith in their necks
Til industry, invention, enterprise, sound sense and power!
Mercie, whit a collection of awfie words
First thing in the morning, tae!
Tycoons tak ower frae the bards and lauchin lassies,
Hairt liggs doun at feet of Gowden Cauf
Enslaved by the muckler god of day,
King Sol the Affluent, Giver of Riches, credits, yachts,
(And *poules de luxe, parbleu!*), wha at his rising
Raises man to stark endeavour, dull as ditch,
And at his setting sets him free to play
And dream and plan and dream again
And waste his substance in the fleein spree
And argy-bargle like the Hula Bird
Round and round, backlins foremaist,
In aye-decreasing concentric circles
Till you ken what—
And seek and dream and fecht—and love whiles—
All things ither being equal, o' course.

hain—preserve; *spreit*—spirit; *greit*—weep; *slocken my drouth*—slake my
thirst; *biding*—staying; *sain*—bless; *hap*—cover; *haill*—whole; *unflichter-
ing*—unfluttering; *lichtless airt*—lightless direction; *blythsome*—merry;
haud—hold; *muckle-mou*—big-mouth; *cap*—cup; *bummer*—manager; *pits*
—puts; *her lane*—alone; *dawin yesternicht*—dawning last night; *gin*—if;

saumon-reid—salmon-red; *athort*—across; *luift*—sky; *daunert*—strolled; *sel*—self; *kyte*—belly; *dune*—done; *aa*—all; *aft agley*—often awry; *clopperin*—clip-clopping; *gey near*—very near; *the Auld Kirk's dug*—the same again; *we'se*—we shall; *bittie*—little while; *lith*—crick; *awfie*—awful; *lauchin lassies*—laughing girls; *liggs*—lies; *Gowden Cauf*—Golden Calf; *muckler*—bigger; *fleein spree*—drunken jolification; *argy-bargle*—argue; *backlins foremaist*—backside foremost; *fecht*—fight; *whiles*—at times.

ROBERT TAIT b. *1943*

THE MONSTER
(Dedicated to the observers on the shores of Loch Ness)

Some Scots Guards lie strangled in their kilts but it's all right
  they're only dolls. Edinburgh Castle has dissolved
  because someone put too much sugar in the mixture.

I cross George Street to meet some friends in the rain but they
  slant into the ground dead bored in front of the Edinburgh
  Bookshop. And when a man from *The Sunday Times* offers
  me a Festival Issue,

What can I say but it's too late, the city's already sunk
  into the cavities of its buildings, and the Nor'loch is
  seeping back. The Nor'loch is seeping back, brown as the
  colour of old paintings especially in the corners where
  they're nearly

Black. What with the rain and the haar and the sea and
  the clouds, the perfect human profiles do not fool me :
  they too are only figures in water only
  for a moment still. What is here is

Ungoverned, still has prehistoric monstrous forms is not
  recognised as having hunted in clans raped divided ruled

236

not recognised in the watery shadows of lawyers on the
mound the uncontrollable forms of senseless killers is not
permitted even its flower power.

No one is talking about it, wondering when it will gain its
independence. Alice fell to her wonderland or death through
the grains of what perfectly represented a dining room
which didn't seem to change, likewise in the night round its
dark lapping empty centre

The new space city of Edinburgh hangs in its cold, sound-tracks
cut off, lights far away as stars zooming like atoms through
day-shapes of office–castles and sticky rock. Lonely women
in the sky now inexplicably sob (signals seeping through
the spaces), faintly, like transistors, soft.

LANDSCAPE

With the natural gaiety of someone scratching himself
    I turn on the television and, an abstracted
    smile on my face,
    turn
    slowly :
    distracted by the window, which, full of animated
    diagrams of botany, records that President
    Novotny has been eased out by some internal pressure.

But just look at this landscape! Today
there are sets designed like pebbles,
like handbags or briefcases, or they
lie around like small unmarked gravestones.
    Voices hover or
    slide over them
    or sit in your lap

in the most innocent way.
I am aware only of the colours
that make this familiar
landscape familiar:

I forget the internal pressures, the ghostliness and deaths
the colours and voices survive. I forget even that the television
is there and take on (I imagine) a gently growing smile as I watch
fruit expand, oranges peel and glow, their rind shred
and knit
fine blond hair,
their skin become the skin
of a delicately tinted girl, whose breasts shine
in the sun whose sex with its hair—
fine lines, however, always fades to a distant sound
of music and
the whitest shade
of absence.

SCOTTISH COUNTRY DANCE MUSIC

Here no one even talks, the faces on the screen will not move at
    all for anyone, the Algerian whose act consisted of laughing
    his face into fantastic sculptures is gone, Jimmy Shand
    ("Smiler") stands just off the edge of his band, watching
    waves?

He moves his slab of a music box back and forward between his
    hands, his face i.e. one side of his head scored in low relief
    is steady, much smaller than the big squared kilt that hangs
    across his legs in the middle of the screen, an interlude
    sign that's what it is, that's him

On TV, and his band so still the music winds over them or falls in

sheets across them, no dancers, only the space of the screen
around them, beyond that the space of a room in which I
sit wondering how often this will be repeated, beyond that
the dark knocked down spaces of Scottish towns

Where things so seldom grow in crowds as any daffodils found in
Glasgow Polmont Falkirk Queenzieburn or Bonnybridge
always show, and beyond that the darkest spaces of the
moors where no one goes at all except perhaps to
masturbate or kill the birds, and the lochs where monsters

Are heard of but surface only like clouds & finally the mountains
that echo the shapes of the ear, plenty of space for a music
that must be repeated till it fills everywhere with itself,
invisible, and even empties its world of its dancers in the
end, you are listening to

Jimmy Shand and his band, Jimmy Shand the music man, he stands
(always stands) in dead silence and would rather not appear,
mixes to the quiet man huddled in his car eating fish by a
beach drifting home then through the dark, who will shortly
disappear.

In Cumnock on the edge of the mines the miners talked or drank.
Bel Vox or Vegas, jukeboxes with wrap-round windscreens,
their wheels and wings tucked under them, stood glowing
in the corners of almost empty cafes, but it was the sound of

Jimmy Shand that crossed the street to the pub or came through
grilles in the ceiling like gas, I don't recall the miners' faces,
only their drawl, their drone and their hands with lost
fingers, they were gentle as hard-men riding featureless
ranges

On the edge of total darkness, riding so long they no longer feel
themselves move, their gun-hands scattered small change
as time went in quiet pints, the dark windows of the old-

fashioned Co-op stores grew dustier, no unions marched and

Sang, the TV screens dwindled to cold white spots while above
black mines with their tiny lights the stars blip in the dark
like a vast council housing scheme, this is the great hang-up
here no one talks, you remember reels, or are hearing them,
and your chair rocks just off the edge of space.

Mayday 68.

DERICK THOMSON b. 1921

CRUAIDH?

Cuil-lodair, is Briseadh na h-Eaglaise,
is briseadh nan tacannan—
lamhachas-làidir dà thriane de ar comas;
'se seòltachd tha dhìth oirnn.
Nuair a theirgeas a' chruaidh air faobhar na speala
caith bhuat a' chlach-lìomhaidh;
chan eil agad ach iarunn bog
mur eil de churas 'nad innleachd na ni sgathadh.

Is caith bhuat briathran mìne
oir chan fhada bhios briathran agad;
tha Tuatha Dé Danann fo'n talamh,
tha Tìr nan Og anns an Fhraing,
's nuair a ruigeas tu Tìr a' Gheallaidh,
mura bi thu air t' aire,
coinnichidh Sasunnach riut is pìlon air,
a dh' innse dhut gun tug Dia, bràthair athar, còir dha anns
an fhearann.

STEEL?

Culloden, the Disruption, and the breaking up of the tack-farms—two-thirds of our power is violence; it is cunning we need. When the tempered steel near the edge of the scythe-blade is worn, thrown away the whetstone; you have nothing left but soft iron unless your intellect has a steel edge that will cut clean.

And throw away soft words, for soon you will have no words left; the Fathers of the Faery are underground, the Country of the Ever-young is in France, and when you reach the Promised Land, unless you are on your toes, a bland Englishman will meet you, and say to you that God, his uncle, has given him a title to the land.

SRATH NABHAIR

Anns an adhar dhubh-ghorm ud,
àirde na sìorraidheachd os ar cionn,
bha rionnag a' priobadh ruinn
's i freagairt mireadh an teine
ann an cabair tigh m' athar
a' bhliadhna thugh sinn an tigh le bleideagan sneachda.

Agus sud a' bhliadhna cuideachd
a shlaod iad a' chailleach do'n t-sitig,
a shealltainn cho eòlach 's a bha iad air an Fhìrinn,
oir bha nid aig eunlaith an adhair
(agus cròthan aig na caoraich)
ged nach robh àit aice-se anns an cuireadh i a ceann fòidhpe.

A Shrath Nabhair 's a Shrath Chill Donnain,
is beag an t-iongnadh ged a chinneadh am fraoch àluinn oirbh,

241

a' falach nan lotan a dh' fhàg Padraig Sellar 's a sheòrsa,
mar a chunnaic mi uair is uair boireannach cràbhaidh
a dh' fhiosraich dòrainn an t-saoghail-sa
is sìth Dhé 'na sùilean.

STRATHNAVER

In that blue-black sky, as high above us as eternity, a star was winking at us, answering the leaping flames of fire in the rafters of my father's house, that year we thatched the house with snowflakes.

And that too was the year they hauled the old woman out on to the dung-heap, to demonstrate how knowledgeable they were in Scripture, for the birds of the air had nests (and the sheep had folds) though she had no place in which to lay down her head.

O Strathnaver and Strath of Kildonan, it is little wonder that the heather should bloom on your slopes, hiding the wounds that Patrick Sellar, and such as he, made, just as time and again I have seen a pious woman who has suffered the sorrow of this world, with the peace of God shining from her eyes.

TROIMH UINNEIG A' CHITHE

Nuair tha 'n sneachda mìn so a' tuiteam,
a' streap gu sàmhach ris na h-uinneagan,
a' mirean air sruthan na h-iarmailt,
ga chàrnadh fhéin ri gàrraidhean

'na chithean sàr-mhaiseach,
is mo mhac 'na leum le aoibhneas,
chi mi 'na shùilean-san greadhnachas gach geamnradh
a thainig a riamh air mo dhaoine :
faileas an t-sneachda an sùilean m' athar,
's mo sheanair 'na bhalach a' ribeadh dhìdeigean.

Is chi mi troimh uinneig a' chithe so,
's anns an sgàthan tha mire ris,
am bealach tha bearradh nan linntean
eadar mise, 's mi falbh nan sgàirneach,
agus mo shinnsrean, a muigh air àirigh,
a' buachailleachd chruidh-bainne 's ag òl a' bhlàthaich.
Chi mi faileas an tighean 's am buailtean
air fàire an uaigneis,
's tha sud mar phàirt de mo dhualchas.

Iadsan a' fàgail staid a' bhalaich,
's a' strì ri fearann, 's a' treabhadh na mara
le neart an guaillibh,
's ag adhradh, air uairibh;
is mise caitheamh an spionnaidh, ach ainneamh,
a' treabhadh ann an gainneamh.

WHEN THIS FINE SNOW IS FALLING

When this fine snow is falling, climbing quietly to the
windows, dancing on air-currents, piling itself up against the
walls in lovely drifts, while my son leaps with joy, I see in his
eyes the elation that every winter brought to my people : the
reflection of snow in my father's eyes, and my grandfather as
a boy snaring starlings.

And I see, through the window of this snowdrift, and in the

glass that dancingly reflects it, the hill-pass cutting through the generations that lie between me, on the scree, and my ancestors, out on the shieling, herding milk-cows and drinking buttermilk. I see their houses and fields reflected on the lonely horizon, and that is part of my heritage.

When their boyhood came to an end they strove with the land, and ploughed the sea with the strength of their shoulders, and worshipped, sometimes; I spend their strength, for the most part, ploughing in the sand.

CLANN-NIGHEAN AN SGADAN

An gàire mar chraiteachan salainn
ga fhroiseadh bho 'm bial,
an sàl 's am picil air an teanga,
's na miaran cruinne, goirid a dheanadh giullachd,
no a thogadh leanabh gu socair, cuimir,
seasgair, fallain,
gun mhearachd,
's na sùilean cho domhainn ri fèath.

B'e bun-os-cionn na h-eachdraidh a dh' fhàg iad
'nan tràillean aig ciùrairean cutach,
thall 's a-bhos air Galldachd 's an Sasuinn.
Bu shaillte an duais a thàrr iad
ás na mìltean bharaillean ud,
gaoth na mara geur air an craiceann,
is eallach a' bhochdainn 'nan ciste,
is mara b'e an gàire
shaoileadh tu gu robh an teud briste.

Ach bha craiteachan uaille air an cridhe,
ga chumail fallain,

is bheireadh cutag an teanga
slisinn á fanaid nan Gall—
agus bha obair rompa fhathast
nuair gheibheadh iad dhachaidh,
ged nach biodh maoin ac':
air oidhche robach gheamhraidh,
ma bha sud an dàn dhaibh,
dheanadh iad daoine.

THE HERRING GIRLS

Their laughter like a sprinkling of salt showered from their lips, brine and pickle on their tongues, and the stubby short fingers that could handle fish, or lift a child gently, neatly, safely, wholesomely, unerringly, and the eyes that were deep as a calm.

The topsy-turvy of history had made them slaves to short-arsed curers, here and there in the Lowlands, in England. Salt the reward they won from those thousands of barrels, the sea-wind sharp on their skins, and the burden of poverty in their kists, and were it not for their laughter you might think the harp-string was broken.

But there was a sprinkling of pride on their hearts, keeping them sound, and their tongues' gutting-knife would tear a strip from the Lowlanders' mockery—and there was work awaiting them when they got home, though they had no wealth: on a wild winter's night, if that were their lot, they would make men.

Duin àrd, tana
's fiasag bheag air,
's locair 'na làimh :
gach uair theid mi seachad
air bùth-shaoirsneachd sa' bhaile,
's a thig gu mo chuimhne fàileadh na min-sàibh,
thig gu mo chuimhne cuimhne an àit ud,
le na cisteachan-laighe,
na h-ùird 's na tairgean,
na sàibh 's na sgeilbean,
is mo sheanair crom,
is sliseag bho shliseag ga locradh
bho'n bhòrd thana lom.

Mus robh fhios agam dé bh' ann bàs;
beachd, bloigh fios, boillsgeadh
de'n dorchadas, fathann de'n t-sàmhchair.
'S nuair a sheas mi aig uaigh,
là fuar Earraich, cha dainig smuain
thugam air na cisteachan-laighe
a rinn esan do chàch :
'sann a bha mi 'g iarraidh dhachaidh,
far am biodh còmhradh, is tea, is blàths.

Is anns an sgoil eile cuideachd,
san robh saoir na h-inntinn a' locradh,
cha tug mi 'n aire do na cisteachan-laighe,
ged a bha iad 'nan suidhe mun cuairt orm;
cha do dh' aithnich mi 'm bréid Beurla,
an lìomh Gallda bha dol air an fhiodh,
cha do leugh mi na facail air a' phràis,
cha do thuig mi gu robh mo chinneadh a' dol bàs.
Gus an dainig gaoth fhuar an Earraich-sa

a locradh a' chridhe;
gus na dh' fhairich mi na tairgean a' dol tromham,
's cha shlànaich tea no còmhradh an cràdh.

COFFINS

A tall thin man with a short beard, and a plane in his hand:
whenever I pass a joiner's shop in the city, and the scent of saw-
dust comes to my mind, memories return of that place, with the
coffins, the hammers and nails, saws and chisels, and my grand-
father, bent, planing shavings from a thin, bare plank.

Before I knew what death was; or had any notion, a glimmer-
ing of the darkness, a whisper of the stillness. And when I stood
at his grave, on a cold Spring day, not a thought came to me of
the coffins he made for others: I merely wanted home where
there would be talk, and tea, and warmth.

And in the other school also, where the joiners of the mind
were planing, I never noticed the coffins, though they were
sitting all round me; I did not recognise the English braid, the
Lowland varnish being applied to the wood, I did not read the
words on the brass, I did not understand that my race was dying.
Until the cold wind of this Spring came to plane the heart; until
I felt the nails piercing me, and neither tea nor talk will heal
the pain.

SYDNEY TREMAYNE b. 1912

A SENSE OF BALANCE

Riding, erect and solemn, his twenty-six-year-old bicycle,
Spats revolving in slow motion with the rat trap pedals,

Our father, bearing his ample umbrella perpendicular,
Ruled on the rainy road a wake of comparative dryness
As he moved in his dignity through the slate roofed town.

THE HARE

In the split woods a broken sapling,
Cold catkins that I stoop below.
Explosion of a blackbird's wings
Kicks up exclamatory snow.

Silence, the burden of the song,
Resumes where winds have blasted through.
The white fields swell to the dark sky,
The matrix they are frozen to.
Stopped in my fiftieth winter's track
I see the maze a March hare ran.
This wilderness supports a hare;
It also may support a man.

ELEMENTS AND ADAPTATIONS

A rook climbs down the wind step after step
Yet overshoots the catapulting tree,
Takes the invisible escalator up
And sails in weightless orbit round the sky.

A trout flies in fast water, hovering
Firm as a kestrel in the pushing stream,
Vibrating tail, fins quick as a snake's tongue,
Tonnage of water rumbling like a drum.

248

Men in their gale of chances unforeseen,
Anchored by apparatus, tug and strain,
Also break out of nature's neat design
To pot the moon with a precise machine.

THE FOX

A vision of silence startled me:
A sinuous fox lightfooting past my door.
Out of the corner of his yellow eye
Glanced round his shoulder. Seeing nothing there,
Skirted the tall dry biscuit coloured grass
Unhurriedly, choosing the open way;
Like an hallucination passed across
To spring the trap forgotten many a day.

One who was brave and frightened, fugitive,
Fox coloured hair, eyes full of level flames,
Leaps out of buried memory to live,
The brightest thing in daylight. Swiftly comes
The verbal thought how many years she's dead.
The fox has slipped away in the dense wood.

INEVITABILITY

Sun, pale tissue paper, cannot light
The mist that is a travesty of white.
The dark is coming soon without a day,
And this is not what I had meant to say.

No. I was thinking how I sell my time
As millions must, reasoning without rhyme,
How the queer labour that the world requires
Is poking ashes without lighting fires.

The sun is cold, caught in a standing cloud.
Nonsense. So high the clouds are not allowed
And no one there makes poems, for the heat.
There is more life to waste in every street.

O life, O sun, O nonsense, and O time.
When past the missing stairs like spores we climb
In such combustion we participate
As fires the rose to its determined state.

STORY FOR IMPERIALISTS

My father's father's sword, hung on the wall,
Was blunt in fact and ceremonial.
I'd borrow it in secret, draw it out,
Lunge at a tree with full five stone of weight,
Watch the blade curve and whip back straight.
Nothing I tried could even burr the point.
I claimed its virtues, growing confident,
Squinting with narrow exaltation, rather
As though to close one eye to fact and father.
Yet my small son has snapped this blade in half
Like a dry stick, a rotten staff,
Not in romantic emulation,
But digging worms with Freudian fascination.
The hilt lies in my hand. A broken blade,
Appropriate enough, leads no crusade,
And in a dustbin shall be laid,
False prop of the imagination's games,

Burdened with father's father's father's names.

EXPLOSIVE DUST

What is done is done, is done
Shouts the starling in the sun.
Belsen's buried in the brain.
Roots that thirst like weasels rip
Earth and what earth covers up.
Every crime and more to come
Is the promise of each time
Yet the world outlives the lot.
Generations are on heat:
In shining ignorance like flame
The newest creatures, without blame,
Rise in vigour of their blood
To stalk each other through the wood.
Constantly the world disowns
Canting sermons upon stones
And consumes its rotten bones.
Mind draws nothing, the sun must,
From the past's explosive dust.

EARTH SPIRITS

The leveret in the leaves
Eating forget-me-nots freshly in bloom,
Pulling the heads off and reversing them
Fastidiously, thrives;
Also the weasel thrives, the sleek rat thrives

In this great time of plenty that arrives.

The world of the young hare
Is hairy as his milky mother's teat
Who suckles him and rolls him off his feet,
Licks him with rapid care,
Then leaves him with a leap to his own care
Among forget-me-nots to sit and stare.

Staring through sunlit hours
As in a dream, his harebrained vision flies
Over the fields, alert how the land lies
Outside the bed of flowers.
Not to be found but find, for instance, flowers
Is fortune in this Eden set with snares.

Colour of earth, alone
Almost from birth, hares when they reach full size
Leer out of landscapes like sardonic spies,
Hares that are closer kin
To tuft and stone than to their nearest kin,
And hold their ground by knowing where to run.

MIXED WEATHER

The holly leaves are glinting in the sun.
Thumped by the wind half senseless we come in,
Into our wits and out of part of our senses,
To watch how the light dances
And lie to ourselves that the long winter's done.

The naked trees roll wildly. Hedges lean
Ready to take off smartly from the scene.
Shadows, dead leaves and flurries of snow are flying.

252

All fixity's for denying
And wind blurts at the door like a trombone.

Forty-foot cherry trees lie on the ground
Roots raised like horns, no more to be earthbound.
The sky is blue and white and dark and glowing.
A rock in the tide's flowing,
The hill is hit by wave upon wave of sound.

At last the sun goes down, an orange blaze,
And night takes over with a darker noise.
My collie dog who wags his tail in sleeping
Feels he is in safe keeping
Lacking the fearful forethought we call wise.

Lock the door, trusting that it won't blow in.
Hear how the world's alive. The haring moon
Breaks cover and goes tearing into space,
Space that is like packed ice
With all the furies yelling out of tune.

ANNE TURNER b. 1925

DEMOLITION AND CONSTRUCTION

Up where the roof had been, the debonair
danger-money boys, working with tools and trust,
attacked each stone they balanced on, then just
as it toppled, they'd kick up and land square
on the very ledge it fell from and prepare
to prise this foothold too. Exploding dust,
the stones hurled one by one, and thrust on thrust
the skyline dancers flickered in the air.
Now where they teetered, shoppers scuff and pause,

worried, at price-tags or a maker's name,
though on these carpets, flabby muscles cause
no sort of mischance—a mere slip won't maim,
nor all the bargaining that ever was
devise such balance in the money game.

MEDUSA

The ageing woman combs her hair
much as she did when, in her prime,
fashion and custom captured her.
And all her thought reflects that time.

Thought reflects that time for her
is a hair-spring; is defeat
spiralling within the coils
of static movement, self-deceit.

Movement, self-deceit, surrounds
the car, the clothes, the views expressed.
One moment between youth and age
matured, and prophesied the rest:

prophesied the rust, the dust—
the last mutations in her veins.
She struggles, prisoner of whims
which no platonic lust sustains.

Must so stains the well-dressed act
that *why* is lost beneath what seems.
A ghost virginity presides
wistfully over dyes and creams.

Cries and dreams, corroding cares,

wrinkle the mask to mock despair:
a myth that shames the mirror where
the ageing woman combs her hair.

LAPSE

Our clock has company tonight—
the old chap from next door
sits beside her on the mantelpiece,
and the two of them are hard at it.
They don't get on.
He's a bit slow. So is she,
though she won't admit it.
She thinks she's still
a fast little piece
and clacks along
like a honeymoon mini
with a can tied on.
He has a hiccup in his tick,
ratchets that wheeze with rust,
and the racket he makes
tripping on missing cogs
is setting *her* teeth on edge.
Then the seconds are out!
The bickering quickens,
distracts our talk—we stare
at the blandly magnetic dials
pointing ridiculous moments,
impossible angles of once-upon-
a-time . . . The interlocked
echoes relax. Two hysterical
anachronisms subside,
snickering absently.
—what were we saying?

The fact is, neither of us care
what time it is.

W. PRICE TURNER b. 1927

FABLE FROM LIFE

Eight hundred telephone directories
will bulletproof a truck, claims
a fruit company in South America.
Think of a bullet with so many numbers
on it, stopping nothing. Bandits,
clamped to their rocks like wild posies,
leap up, banging and screeching.
The desert bristles with rifles
and vexed moustaches. After all
that fuss, the truck bumps on.
Fruitless compliments to the patron saint
of tough luck; then a clutter of big hats
raises a thin oasis of ritual smoke.
El Moroso, who once broke a tooth
on his own bullet in the first bite
of cool plunder, savours the loss.
Clearly, the moral is to have no truck
with thick-skinned civilisations.

PERSONAL COLUMN

In daydream fantasies of self-indulgence
my favourite theme is the scene where
I walk into a room loaded with innocence

to be the victim of an orgy there.

The background varies, but my home will do,
where I am greeted by five lady guests,
or a strange hotel, a midnight interview:
and I gasp helpless under dabbling breasts.

Why do I stage intrigues of such dimension,
always eager to be outnumbered in the deed?
For the carnal fact is, I hasten to mention,
that I would never deny a lady in need.

When Ladies' Circles invite me to remote spots,
I accept with alacrity and warm suspicion.
I leave my door unlocked and cook in my thoughts,
but not one nymphomaniac seeks admission.

So damn all those lousy novelists who instil
sex as a fillip, larkin' around like fizz,
which makes one hanker for the pay-off thrill:
a little taste of how Orpheus got his.

SELECT CIRCLES

These educated snake-charmers
with their lacquered wicker baskets
and two finger tunes, are a riot
performing in little groups.

It is a kind of jazz they play,
an ungobbling of endless spaghetti:
the first man to fill his plate
siphons his pet to take a bow.

So the hinged lid rises and the joke
snake wobbles its hood and nods
like a ball bobbing on a spray
while all the crooked tongues sway too.

Each fakir solos and subsides;
now I recall the bright school prank
of popping carbide in inkwells.
Anything to gain attention.

For one of these smooth trick items
you can snap the catch on quick,
a house-trained phantom ripe to rise
and fall for the same shrill pitch,

on bad days I'd swop my own
old bone-crusher of a python,
if I knew any way out of this
damn pit I dug to keep him in.

REPROACHES

They are pulling down that London hotel
where I slept alone in a double bed
rather than deny my half of the dream.

A new Labour Exchange has been opened
to accommodate those people I put off
to see you, on days when you could not come.

The swans no longer bother to patrol
the lake in the park, and those small flowers
you were fond of have been taken away.

After the Haydn symphony, the man
with the baton announced there was no point
in playing Mahler to your empty seat.

Now the post office has decided to suspend
deliveries, and they can blow up
the rest of the world too, for all I care.

ROAD HOG

A zoo for the ego, on wheels
to convey its zodiac of hungers.

Dogs can be trained to beg
if that retreating stagger pleases.
Apes will wave spoons or brushes,
and bears have danced in chains.

But these faces caged in windscreens
now, they crawl with impatience
to go leaping through flaming hoops
at some intangible sustenance.

Love was yesterday's ill-digested morsel;
roll on, the next! The brutal fist
that selects a button once controlled
a shuddering chariot.

Now, in his playpen battering-ram,
enraged at everything that stands
on its own twolegs, he can charge
down the open road through the ever-changing
challenge of unresisting scenery,
sure of this armoured animal

he monitors, from horn to tail-light,
a devil moving with the times.

DRIVEN AT NIGHT

With another man's wife I share space
in the back of another man's car.
This is the only life I've got
and here I am staking it
on another's skill and care.
There's no shaking it,
he drives well. Beside me, she seems
to sleep as lights caress her face.
If this is lust, I'm slaking it
by courtesy of her dreams.
But I know my place:
there's no mistaking it,
even when that fat pimp, the moon,
contrives to dwell on her flesh, making it
seem unreal by some remote amendment.
We'll be free, separately, soon,
of this shut-in moving mesh
that has me taking it
seriously. Here is the tenth commandment,
and this is Bill Turner breaking it.

FULL SUPPORTING PROGRAMME

Just at the most exciting part
of the film, as the secret agent
hiding in the coffin pushed up the lid——

suddenly behind us a woman screaming!
We followed the direction, turned heads miming
disgust: she had ruptured our paid-for dream.
Meanwhile, back on the screen, sinister
extras lurked in the vaults that took
half a day to light. We saw what a crude
bit of cutting did for a poor script.
But she was at it again: "Help
me! I think my husband 's dead!"
Sure enough, there was a dark
heap in the seat beside her. What
a way to go, before you even
know what 's on next week. But there was little
we could do; it was the manager's
problem. Bad for business, that. The actors
were leaping out on one another. Behind,
a nice bit part for a Nightingale usherette.
Luckily the heroine in a bikini
appeared in time to save her lover, because
there were only five minutes left to blow
up the castle and sell us ice-cream.
Next time I thought about it
a boy who looked too young to see
the main feature sat where the shrieker
had been. We left while a priest was easing
into the corpse's seat, his folded coat
carefully trailing across the lap
of the mesmerised boy, as more
death and seduction began.

ONE FOR THE ROAD

Take a thousand hearses, bumper to bumper,
crawling the highway, a jolly Bank Holiday,
parping and beeping, egos in every key,

and imagine yourself in the last queue for death,
sweating and swatting flies and cursing the lights,
when word comes down the line—Famous Actor
Dies—and the wheels turn as it registers
while you cover six feet or so and brake.
In the space it takes for a tar blister to boil
and burst as you press on they are mourning
the ex-king of some foreign stamp or other,
and at the cross-roads the Pope passes away
making a sort of sign which you shrug off
much as the prone unknown pedestrian lets slip
his patched tarpaulin of identity.
One man's death magnifies its witnesses,
the deaths of many diminish only death.
A thousand cans on a slow conveyor belt
to the bright label obliterating all,
the cars obediently jiggle along.
Now consider yourself smack in the middle
with a fool in front and a maniac behind
when the good philosopher goes dazzled
into the dark: check all your instruments.
The report of a great writer's gun backfires
along trails of rubber teeth; echoes whine
from the distant toll-bridge. You have a map?
Of course. But the road changes even as you steer.
Ditches are wider, milestones bob up like rabbits
becoming tombstones as you peer ahead, landmarks
veer off to anonymous horizons, bulldozers
nudge rubble; only the clear paths of the mind
stay clean. So take this and drive it hard and deep
into your own right of way. Can you say
by what deaths you came here? You can not.
You have forgotten whatever you may mean, geared
to the motives of your weird machine, bent forward
listening more and more to that queer ascending
inner amplification of a sound
like the roar of a thousand voices without fear.

THE HERON

China, Xth century, when Siu Hi
painted his Heron of the Snows
on a Frost-covered Branch

the ungainly, cold-eyed bird
the mass of white plumage against
the grey sky, the uncouth claws

and Tchouang-tzu asked : what
does the great bird see that can rise
so high in the wind? Is it original

matter whirling in a dust of atoms?
the air that gives life to creatures?
the unnamed force that moves the worlds?

on a riven branch, the heron
like the ghost of an answer

balances in the wind
and stares at the questioning world

ACKNOWLEDGMENTS

For permission to include uncollected poems, thanks are due to James Aitchison, J. K. Annand, D. M. Black, Alan Bold, George Mackay Brown, George Bruce, Tom Buchan, Stewart Conn, James Copeland, Robin Fulton, Robert Garioch, Flora Garry, Duncan Glen, Eric Gold, Giles Gordon, W. S. Graham, Alan Jackson, Laughton Johnston, John Kincaid, T. S. Law, George Macbeth, Hugh Macdiarmid, Alastair Mackie, Alasdair Maclean, Sorley Maclean, Joseph Macleod, William Montgomerie, Edwin Morgan, Ken Morrice, Alan Riddell, R. Crombie Saunders, Tom Scott, Charles Senior, Mrs Marie Singer, Iain Crichton Smith, Sydney Goodsir Smith, Robert Tait, Anne Turner, W. Price Turner, to the Byron Press for poems by G. S. Fraser.

For work from collections, thanks are due to Akros Publications, for poems by George Bruce, Maurice Lindsay, Edwin Morgan, Stephen Mulrine and Alexander Scott; to Barrie & Rockliff, for poems by Tom Buchan; to Brookside Press, for poems by Maurice Lindsay; to Jonathan Cape for a poem by Kenneth White; to Caithness Books, for poems by David Morrison and Charles Senior; to Chatto & Windus and The Hogarth Press, for poems by Alan Bold, George Mackay Brown, Norman MacCaig and Sydney Tremayne; to Edinburgh University Press, for poems by Edwin Morgan; to Eyre & Spottiswoode, for poems by Iain Crichton Smith; to Faber & Faber for poems by Douglas Dunn; to Fulcrum Press, for poems by Alan Jackson; to Gairm Publications, for poems by Donald Macaulay and Derick Thomson; to Hutchinson for poems by Stewart Conn and Alan Riddell; to Linden Press for poems by Maurice Lindsay; to M. Macdonald for poems by J. K. Annand, Helen B. Cruickshank, Robin Fulton, Robert Garioch, Ken Morrice and Sydney Goodsir Smith; to Macmillan for poems by George Macbeth; to Outposts Publications for poems by Laughton Johnston; to Rupert Hart-Davis for poems by Sydney Tremayne; to Scorpion Press for poems by D. M. Black and George Macbeth; to Turret Books for a poem by Giles Gordon; to Villiers Publications for poems by W. Price Turner.

Thanks are also due to the magazine *Akros*, *Gairm* and *Lines Review*, and to the *Scottish Poetry* annuals.

CONTRIBUTORS' VERSE PUBLICATIONS SINCE 1959

JAMES AITCHISON. Contributor to the first three numbers of the annual anthology *Scottish Poetry* (Edinburgh University Press, Edinburgh, 1966, 1967, 1968)

J. K. ANNAND. *Sing it Aince for Pleisure* (M. Macdonald, Edinburgh, 1965); *Two Voices* (M. Macdonald, Edinburgh, 1968)

D. M. BLACK. *With Decorum* (Scorpion Press, London, 1967); *A Dozen Short Poems* (Turret Books, 1968); *The Educators* (Barrie & Rockliff: The Cresset Press, 1969)

ALAN BOLD. *Society Inebrious* (Mowat Hamilton, Edinburgh, 1965); *The Voyage* (M. Macdonald, Edinburgh, 1966); *To Find the New* (Chatto & Windus: The Hogarth Press, London, 1967); *A Perpetual Motion Machine* (Chatto & Windus: The Hogarth Press, London, 1969); *The State of the Nation* (Chatto & Windus: The Hogarth Press, London, 1969)

GEORGE MACKAY BROWN. *Loaves and Fishes* (The Hogarth Press, London, 1959); *The Year of the Whale* (Chatto & Windus: The Hogarth Press, London, 1965); *The Five Voyages of Arnor* (K. D. Duval, Edinburgh, 1966); *Orkney Tapestry* (Gollancz, London, 1969)

GEORGE BRUCE. *Landscape and Figures* (Akros Publications, Preston, 1967). Co-editor of *Scottish Poetry* anthologies

TOM BUCHAN. *Dolphins at Cochin* (Barrie & Rockliff: The Cresset Press, London, 1969)

STEWART CONN. *The Chinese Tower* (M. Macdonald, Edinburgh, 1967); *Thunder in the Air* (Akros Publications, Preston, 1967); *Stoats in the Sunlight* (Hutchinson, London, 1968)

JAMES COPELAND. Contributor to B.B.C. radio

HELEN B. CRUICKSHANK. *The Ponnage Pool* (M. Macdonald, Edinburgh, 1968)

DOUGLAS DUNN. *Terry Street* (Faber & Faber, London, 1969)

G. S. FRASER. *Conditions* (The Byron Press, Nottingham, 1969)

ROBIN FULTON. *A Manner of Definition* (Giles Gordon, London, 1963); *An Italian Quartet* (London Magazine Editions, London, 1966); *Instances* (M. Macdonald, Edinburgh, 1967); Blok's *The Twelve* (Akros Publications, Preston, Lancashire, 1968); *Inventories* (Caithness Books, Thurso, 1969). Editor of *Lines* poetry magazine (M. Macdonald, Loanhead, Midlothian)

ROBERT GARIOCH. *Selected Poems* (M. Macdonald, Edinburgh, 1966). Co-editor of *Scottish International* quarterly

FLORA GARRY. 'Village Magdalen' appeared in *Akros* poetry magazine (vol. 1, no. 3, August 1966) and in *Scottish Poetry 3* (1968)

DUNCAN GLEN ('Ronald Eadie Munro'). *Stanes* (The Author, Preston, 1966); *Idols: when Alexander our King was Dead* (Akros Publications, Preston, 1967); *Kythings* (Caithness Books, Thurso, 1969); *Sunny Summer Sunday Afternoon in the Park?* (Akros Publications, Preston, 1969). Editor of *Akros* poetry magazine and publisher of Akros Publications

ERIC GOLD. *Parklands Poets No. 1* (Akros Publications, Preston, 1969)

GILES GORDON. *Two and Two Make One* (Akros Publications, Preston, 1966); *Two Elegies* (Turret Books, London, 1968)

W. S. GRAHAM. *Malcolm Mooney's Land* (Faber & Faber, London, 1970)

ALAN JACKSON. *Underwater Wedding* (The Author, Edinburgh, 1961); *Well, Ye Ken Noo* (The Author, Edinburgh, 1963); *All Fall Down* (The Kevin Press, Edinburgh, 1965); *The Worstest Beast* (The Kevin Press, Edinburgh, 1967); *The Grim Wayfarer* (Fulcrum Press, London, 1969)

LAUGHTON JOHNSTON. *Meetings* (Outposts Publications, London, 1968)

JOHN KINCAID. Contributor to *Akros* poetry magazine

T. S. LAW. Contributor to *Akros* and *Lines* poetry magazines.

MAURICE LINDSAY. *Snow Warning* (Linden Press, Arundel, 1962); *One Later Day* (The Brookside Press, London, 1964); *This Business of Living* (Akros Publications, Preston, 1969). Co-editor of the *Scottish Poetry* anthologies

DONALD MACAULAY. *Seobhrach As A' Chlaich* (Gairm Publications, Glasgow, 1968)

GEORGE MACBETH. *Lecture to the Trainees* (Fantasy Press, Oxford, 1962); *The Broken Places* (Scorpion Press, Lowestoft, 1963); *A Doomsday Book* (Scorpion Press, Lowestoft, 1965); *The Colour of Blood* (Macmillan, London, 1967); *The Night of Stones* (Macmillan, London, 1968); *A War Quartet* (Macmillan, London, 1969)

NORMAN MACCAIG. *A Common Grace* (Chatto & Windus: The Hogarth Press, London, 1960); *A Round of Applause* (Chatto & Windus: The Hogarth Press, London, 1962); *Measures* (Chatto & Windus: The Hogarth Press, London, 1965); *Surroundings* (Chatto & Windus: The Hogarth Press, London, 1966); *Rings on a Tree* (Chatto & Windus: The Hogarth Press, London, 1968); *A Man in My Position* (Chatto & Windus: The Hogarth Press, London, 1969)

HUGH MACDIARMID. *Collected Poems* (Macmillan, New York, 1962); *A Lap of Honour* (MacGibbon & Kee, London, 1967); *A Clyack-Sheaf* (MacGibbon & Kee, London, 1969)

ALASTAIR MACKIE. *Soundings* (Akros Publications, Preston, 1966)

ALASDAIR MACLEAN. Twenty-one poems in *Lines* no. 30 (October 1969)

SORLEY MACLEAN. First publication of these poems

JOSEPH MACLEOD. Contributor to *Scottish Poetry 1* and *4* (1966 and 1969)

WILLIAM MONTGOMERIE. 'Triptych of Miniatures' appears here for the first time

EDWIN MORGAN. *Poems from Eugenio Montale* (University of Reading School of Art, Reading, 1959); *Sovpoems* (Migrant Press, Worcester, 1961); *Starryveldt* (Eugen Gomringer Press, Frauenfeld, Switzerland, 1965); *Emergent Poems* (Futura 20 editions, Hansjorg Mayer, 1967); *The Second Life* (Edinburgh University Press, Edinburgh, 1968); *gnomes* (Akros Publications, Preston, 1968); *Proverb Folder* (Openings Press, Woodchester, 1969); *The Horseman's Word* (Akros Publications, Preston, 1970); *The Whittrick* (Akros Publications, Preston, 1970)

KEN MORRICE. *Prototype* (M. Macdonald, Edinburgh, 1965)

DAVID MORRISON. *The Saxon Toon* (M. Macdonald, Edinburgh, 1966); *The White Hind* (Caithness Books, Thurso, 1969)

STEPHEN MULRINE. *Poems by Four Glasgow University Poets* (Akros Publications, Preston, 1967)

ALAN RIDDELL. *Majorcan Interlude* (M. Macdonald, Edinburgh, 1962); *The Stopped Landscape* (Hutchinson, London, 1968)

R. CROMBIE SAUNDERS. Contributor to *Lines* and *Akros* poetry magazines

ALEXANDER SCOTT. *Cantrips* (Akros Publications, Preston, 1968)

TOM SCOTT. *The Ship* (Oxford University Press, Oxford, 1963); *At the Shrine o the Unkent Sodger* (Akros Publications, Preston, 1968)

CHARLES SENIOR. *Selected Poems* (M. Macdonald, Edinburgh, 1966); *Harbingers* (Caithness Books, Thurso, 1969)

BURNS SINGER. *Collected Poems*, edited Walter Keir, forthcoming (Secker & Warburg, London)

IAIN CRICHTON SMITH. *Burn is Aran* (Gairm Publications, Glasgow, 1960); *Thistles and Roses* (Eyre & Spottiswoode, London, 1961); *Deer on the High Hills* (Giles Gordon, London, 1962); *Biobuill is Sansan Reice* (Gairm Publications, Glasgow, 1965); *The Law and the Grace* (Eyre & Spottiswoode, London, 1965); *At Helensburgh* (Queen's University, Belfast, 1968); *From Bourgeois Land* (Gollancz, London, 1969); *Lines* no. 29, June 1969 (sixty-one poems)

SYDNEY GOODSIR SMITH. *Figs and Thistles* (Oliver & Boyd, Edinburgh, 1959); *The Vision of the Prodigal Son* (M. Macdonald, Edinburgh, 1960); *Kynd Kittock's Land* (M. Macdonald, Edinburgh, 1966); *Fifteen Poems and a Play* (Southside Publications, Edinburgh, 1969)

ROBERT TAIT. *Poems by Four Glasgow University Poets* (Akros Publications, Preston, 1967). Co-editor of *Scottish International* quarterly

DERICK THOMSON. *Eadar Samhradh is Foghar* (Gairm Publications, Glasgow, 1967). Editor of the Gaelic quarterly *Gairm*

SYDNEY TREMAYNE. *The Swans of Berwick* (Chatto & Windus:

The Hogarth Press, London, 1962); *The Turning Sky* (Rupert Hart-Davis, London, 1969)

ANNE TURNER. *Sudden Shards* (The Grackle Press, Leeds, 1968)

W. PRICE TURNER. *The Flying Corset* (Villiers Press, London, 1962); *Fables from Life* (Northern House Pamphlet Poets, Leeds, 1966); *More Fables from Life* (Ulsterman Publications, Portrush, 1969)

KENNETH WHITE. *Wild Coal* (Club des Etudiants d'Anglais, Paris, n.d. [?1964]; *The Cold Wind of Dawn* (Cape, London, 1966); *The Most Difficult Area* (Cape, London, 1968)